Pressure
Cooking
Anytime

PRESSURE COOKING ANYTIME

In No Time At All

An All-New Guide to
Pressure Cooking and Canning
from the Mirro Test Kitchen

Golden Press
New York

Western Publishing
Company, Inc.
Racine, Wisconsin

Photography by Victor Scocozza

On the front cover: Chicken Javanese (page 42) with Acorn Squash (page 82),
Meat Loaf (page 47), Vegetable Platter (page 84).
On the back cover: Cioppino (page 24), Chinese Spareribs (page 41), Orange
Custard in Orange Cups (page 106), Cherry Pudding (page 97), Fresh Tomato Sauce (page 123),
Asparagus and Peppers Vinaigrette (page 122).

Printed in the U.S.A. by Western Publishing Company, Inc.
Published by Golden Press, New York, New York.

Library of Congress Catalog Card Number: 77-77297

Golden and Golden Press ® are trademarks of Western Publishing Company, Inc.

Silver-plated chafing dish on page 90 courtesy of Oneida Ltd.

Contents

Introduction

Take a new look at the pressure cooker. It's the made-for-today utensil that offers the busy cook multiple savings . . .

• It saves time. Food cooked in a pressure cooker cooks about three times as fast as the same food cooked by a conventional method.
• It saves energy. Because of the vastly reduced cooking times, pressure cooking naturally saves considerably on the amount of energy expended. Furthermore, the heat level required for cooking is far lower than that called for by conventional methods.
• It saves the nutrients and flavors of foods. Because foods cook so quickly and require a minimum amount of liquid, they naturally retain more of their health-giving nutrients. The short cooking time also helps vegetables, in particular, maintain their bright colors.
• It helps you save money. Lamb shanks, stewing beef, tongue, all kinds of budget-beating meat cuts that traditionally call for long-time simmering or braising can be cooked to fork-tender goodness in minutes instead of hours—without the use of chemical tenderizers. Home canning is another pocketbook pleaser. (In fact, pressure canning is the only method recommended as safe by the U.S. Department of Agriculture for the preservation of low-acid foods—meats, poultry, vegetables.)

The pressure cooker can also help you save many a mealtime situation.

And that's what this book is all about. It's not intended to be a pressure cooking primer nor a care-and-usage manual. (The manufacturer has supplied you with all of that information.) But it is intended to help you take better advantage of all of these savings by offering you a broad range of recipes for all kinds of occasions. You'll find that pressure cooking is not just for vegetables or soups. It's for elegant party meals, for hurry-up breakfasts, for weekend brunches, for family dinners.

Chicken still frozen an hour before dinner? Cut into parts and pre-browned, it can be pressure cooked as Coq au Vin in about 20 minutes.

Unexpected guests? What about Spinach-Stuffed Sole or Chinese Spareribs?

Are quick meals for two your daily after-work challenge? Use your pressure cooker to prepare your entire meal—meat and vegetables in separate foil pouches—at one time and in one pot.

Watching your weight? Cut down on calories with dishes like Curried Lamb Chops and Marmalade Soufflé.

The following chapters will show you how to do all of this—and more. You'll be able to bring many regional and international favorites up to today's tempo with pressure cooker recipes that steam puddings in minutes, that transform economical and nutritious dried beans into a variety of flavorful dishes, that permit you to put up in-season foods quickly and safely.

You'll find that pressure cooking is the "saving-est" kind of cooking. For in addition to saving time, energy, money and nutrition, it also saves the cook.

The Principle of Pressure Cooking
It's really very simple. When you heat water to boiling, the water—and the steam it gives off—reach a temperature of 212° F (at sea level).* No matter how long and hard the water is boiled, the temperature never goes above this point; and the water will simply steam away until the pan is dry.

But a pressure cooker traps that steam and puts it to work. As the liquid in a pressure cooker boils, the pan fills with steam; and that steam forces the gasket to lock the cover on. As the pressure increases, the temperature increases. And the higher the pressure, the higher the temperature. So, at 5 pounds of pressure, the temperature becomes 228° F. At 10 pounds, it is 240° F and at 15 pounds it is 250° F. It is these higher-

---

*At altitudes of 2000 feet or more above sea level, the boiling point of water is less than 212° F. To compensate for this difference, it is necessary to use higher pressures for both cooking and canning. If the recipe directions call for 5 pounds of pressure, then you should use 10 pounds. If they call for 10 pounds, then use 15. If 15 pounds is called for, simply increase the cooking time.

than-boiling-point temperatures that create speed cooking. The pressure generated within the cooker actually drives the heat into the food more than twice as fast as conventional heating methods—and thus speeds the rate at which the food absorbs heat.

Getting to Know the Pressure Cooker
The best introduction to pressure cooking will be found in the manual provided by the manufacturer. Read and re-read this guide. Get to know the parts of the pressure cooker, what they do and how to care for them. You will doubtless find basic directions, helpful cooking charts and even recipes. If you misplace the manual, order a replacement from the manufacturer. (Replacement parts for your cooker may also be ordered from the manufacturer if your dealer does not have them.)

Although there are different brands of pressure cookers, with different features, the same principles of pressure cooking apply to all of them. Some models offer a single pressure setting—15 pounds. While they can be used to cook most foods successfully, they are not recommended for canning.

Other models offer a selective pressure control, which provides the cook with a choice of cooking temperatures. And just as specific temperatures are best for baking certain foods in the oven, specific temperatures are best for cooking certain foods in a pressure cooker.

• **15 Pounds (250° F).** Recommended for fresh and frozen vegetables, dried beans, dried fruits, cereals and soups—foods that are generally considered starchy.

• **10 Pounds (240° F).** Recommended for meats, poultry and seafood—protein foods. While this temperature is still high enough to generate speed-cooking, it is low enough to result in less shrinkage and greater retention of natural juices. (Protein foods can also be cooked at 15 pounds pressure by reducing the cooking time.) Ten pounds is also the correct pressure for canning low-acid foods.

• **5 Pounds (228° F).** Recommended for pasta, custards and most steamed breads and puddings. By shortening the cooking time, it is also possible to steam these foods at 15 pounds. Acid foods, like fruits and tomatoes, are canned at 5 pounds pressure.

Note: Although all of the recipes in this book were developed and tested in a cooker with an automatic pressure control and variable settings, they can also be used in other types of pressure cookers. Every recipe includes the recommended pressure setting and, when feasible, an alternate setting.

Tips for Success
If you're new to pressure cooking or to a new-model pressure cooker, it's best to stick to the recipes supplied by the manufacturer or the recipes in this book before you experiment on your own. That way, you'll become familiar with the cooker, with the pressure settings and with the way different foods are treated. Once you feel comfortable with the cooker, you can adapt your own family favorites to the pleasure of speed cooking. Remember, most foods that can be boiled, steamed, stewed or braised can be adapted to the pressure cooker. Here are some tips and reminders to help:
• Always follow the manufacturer's recommendations for the proper care of the cooker and the best cooking techniques and safeguards.
• Wait until the pressure control begins to jiggle before you start to count the cooking time. As soon as the jiggling begins, lower the heat so that the control jiggles about one to three times a minute for cooking, three or four times a minute for canning. The jiggling indicates that the selected pressure is being maintained. The hissing sound and the slight escape of steam that occur between jiggles is normal. (One of the biggest advantages of a weight-control pressure gauge is that even if the heat is inadvertently left on high, the pressure will not exceed the setting. The control will simply jiggle more vigorously to maintain the selected pressure—it's your signal to reduce the heat.)

• When the cooking time is up, turn off the heat and reduce the pressure in the cooker. (Remember, the cover must never be removed until the pressure is reduced.) With fresh or frozen vegetables, fruits or foods that would not be "jarred" by a quick cooling, run cold water over the cooker to reduce pressure instantly. For meats, soups and bean dishes, let the cooker stand 5 minutes before running cold water over it. For canned foods, let the pressure reduce naturally.

• It's best to brown meats well in an uncovered pan (you can use the open cooker) before pressure cooking them. The browning develops flavor and improves the appearance.

• If the recipe does not turn out satisfactorily, don't blame yourself. There are such great differences in the age and tenderness of meats and vegetables, as well as the size of the pieces, that all cooking times must be considered approximate. It's best to undercook rather than overcook. You can always cook the dish a bit more.

• Do not skimp on the amount of liquid used—be it water, broth, wine or vegetable juices. You need enough liquid to generate the steam that will cook the food. Depending on the type of food and the length of the cooking time, the liquid should probably total about 1 cup in a 2½- or 4-quart cooker and 1½ cups in a 6- or 8-quart size.

• Large pieces of meat, like a roast, should not be pressure cooked from the frozen state. Even though it may get done on the outside, the inside will not be cooked through. Small pieces of frozen foods, such as chops, chicken parts and stew meat, should be partially thawed. The thawing is not necessary to ensure thorough cooking, but because they will not pre-brown satisfactorily if completely frozen.

• Any foods that cook at the same pressure for the same length of time can be cooked together in the pressure cooker. (Food flavors do not mingle in live steam.)

• Many recipes, from main-dish casseroles to desserts, call for the use of metal molds, custard cups, baking dishes or bowls. Some, such as foods in packets, are cooked in containers made of foil. To add versatility to your pressure cooking repertoire, you can use almost any heatproof container you have on hand, providing it fits in the cooker. Just be sure the container really is heatproof. You can be sure of metal, and any glass or earthenware dish that can go in the oven; but do not use plastic or containers of untempered glass. If your individual molds are shallow and your pressure cooker is deep enough, you may be able to place a second layer of molds on another rack. You must allow at least 1 inch headspace at the top and sufficient space between the molds to allow the steam to flow freely.

• Don't experiment with applesauce, rhubarb, cranberries, pearl barley, split peas or pea soup. Manufacturers caution that these foods should not be pressure cooked. They tend to froth up and sometimes block the vent tube. When the vent tube is blocked, pressure may appear to be down, when actually it is not. And no attempt should be made to force open the cover.

• Do keep your pressure cooker handy. The more you see it, the more you'll use it. And the more you use it, the more you'll enjoy its many benefits.

About This Book

The following chapters are arranged as you might go about choosing recipes to meet the needs of your lifestyle. You'll find recipes for two and for twenty, for tight-budget times, for waist-watching, for party meals—all with an international accent on flavor.

Whether you're looking for a basic stock, a hearty main course, a versatile vegetable, a delicate dessert, a holiday steamed bread or a new-fashioned old-style preserve, you'll find your allegiance to the pressure cooker will grow as you learn how much it saves for you.

You'll discover that the pressure cooker is one of the best investments you can make for your kitchen and for you. *Pressure Cooking Anytime in No Time at All* will help you make the most of it.

DINNER
FOR ONE OR TWO

Tailor-made — that's what these meals are. Tailored to your time, tailored to your taste and, best of all, tailored to just the right size. Gone are the days when cooking for one or two meant sticking to costly steaks or chops, or eating the same stew for three days running. Take a tip from the following pages and add streamlined variety to your dinner menus.

Here you will discover how to prepare a complete main meal, every course individually seasoned or sauced, in a single utensil — your pressure cooker. The formula is a matter of common sense. We've simply selected foods that cook at the same pressure for the same length of time — and we've put them in foil packets for easy handling (and, of course, to keep a sauce for the meat from running onto the vegetable).

Follow these menus to get the idea, then mix and match courses on your own. If you use foil packets for your own combinations, be sure to keep the tops open. The packets can be placed side by side on the rack or, if necessary, on top of one another, allowing a 1½-inch headspace at the top of the cooker. Use 1 cup water in a 2½- or 4-quart cooker, 1½ cups water in the 6- or 8-quart size. If your own menu partners call for different cooking times, you can still use a single pressure cooker. Start with the longest-cooking item, then add the other courses in sequence, always reducing the pressure instantly by running cold water over the cooker before removing the cover.

Of course, you can also choose recipes from other chapters in the book and adjust the quantities according to your needs. But remember, no matter what size cooker you use or how little food you cook, the time required for pressure cooking does not change.

Individual Meat Loaves
Spinach Soufflés
Pommes Anna

Individual Meat Loaves

¾ pound ground beef
2 slices bacon, minced
½ cup soft bread crumbs
2 cloves garlic, minced
¼ cup minced onion
½ teaspoon salt
¼ teaspoon each allspice, thyme and
   marjoram
   Pinch each of pepper and sugar
½ cup fresh or frozen cranberries
   (optional)

Spinach Soufflés

1 teaspoon flour
1 teaspoon butter or margarine
½ cup milk
   Pinch each of salt, pepper and
   nutmeg
2 eggs, separated
1 package (10½ ounces) frozen
   chopped spinach, thawed and
   squeezed dry

Pommes Anna

2 medium baking potatoes, peeled
   Pinch each of salt and pepper
4 tablespoons butter or margarine,
   melted

1. Combine beef, bacon, bread crumbs, garlic, onion, seasonings and sugar. Fold in the cranberries, if desired. Spoon half of mixture onto each of two 12-inch squares of lightly greased foil. Shape foil into packets, leaving the tops open.
2. For the soufflés, blend flour and butter to make a smooth paste. Bring milk to a boil in a small saucepan. Stir in the flour-butter paste. Cook, stirring, until sauce is smooth and thickened. Season with salt, pepper and nutmeg.
3. Remove from heat, cool slightly and beat in the egg yolks and spinach.
4. Beat whites until stiff but not dry, and gently but quickly fold into the spinach mixture. Divide between 2 greased 6-ounce custard cups. Cover loosely with foil.

5. Cut potatoes into paper-thin rounds. Season with salt and pepper. Lightly brush the insides of two 6-ounce custard cups with melted butter. Arrange potato slices, overlapping each slightly, on the bottom and all around the inside wall of each cup. (They will stick to the melted butter.) Stack remaining slices in the center, brushing each slice with melted butter. Cover loosely with foil.
6. Pour 1½ cups water into cooker. Arrange packets and custard cups on rack in cooker.
7. Cover, set control at 10 and place over high heat until control jiggles. Reduce heat and cook 15 minutes (or cook at 15 for 12 minutes).
8. Remove from heat and let cool 5 minutes; then run cold water over the cooker to finish reducing pressure.
9. Carefully unwrap the Meat Loaves. Unmold the Spinach Soufflés and the Pommes Anna and serve at once.

Serves 2 (6- or 8-quart cooker).

Stuffed Green Peppers
Mashed Potatoes
Quick Italian Sauce

Stuffed Green Peppers

2 large green peppers
¼ pound ground beef
1 cup cooked rice
2 tablespoons minced onion
1 egg
1 clove garlic, minced
1 tablespoon tomato paste
¼ teaspoon salt
  Pinch of pepper

Mashed Potatoes

2 small baking potatoes, peeled and
  diced
1 tablespoon butter or margarine
½ cup heavy cream or light cream
  Salt and pepper

Quick Italian Sauce

1 can (8 ounces) stewed tomatoes
2 cloves garlic, peeled
1 stalk celery, coarsely chopped
1 tablespoon tomato paste
¼ teaspoon each thyme and oregano

1. Slice top from the peppers and scoop out the seeds. Mix beef, rice, onion, egg, garlic, tomato paste, salt and pepper. Fill peppers and wrap in a foil packet, leaving the top open.
2. Place potatoes on a 12-inch square of foil and top with butter. Shape foil into a packet, leaving the top open. Reserve cream, salt and pepper.
3. Combine sauce ingredients in a blender or food mill and puree until smooth. Line a bowl with a large piece of foil and pour in sauce. Wrap ends of foil up and over sauce to form a packet with the top slightly open.
4. Pour 1 cup water into cooker. Place the 3 packets on rack in cooker.
5. Cover, set control at 15 and place over high heat until control jiggles. Reduce heat and cook 13 minutes (or cook at 10 for 16 minutes).
6. Run cold water over the cooker to reduce pressure instantly.

7. Remove peppers to heated serving plate; pour sauce into a heated sauceboat; mash potatoes with cream and season with salt and pepper.

Serves 2 (2½- or 4-quart cooker).
For a 6- or 8-quart cooker, use 1½ cups water in Step 4.

Quick Pot Roast
Braised Carrots
Steamed Parsley Potatoes

Quick Pot Roast

¾ pound beef chuck or round, cut
  into ¼-inch slices
1 tablespoon Worcestershire sauce
2 tablespoons tomato sauce
  Pinch each of salt and pepper

Braised Carrots

2 medium carrots, cut into sticks
1 tablespoon butter or margarine
1 tablespoon sesame seed
1 teaspoon brown sugar
  Pinch each of salt and pepper

Steamed Parsley Potatoes

1 large baking potato, peeled and
  cut into eighths
1 tablespoon butter or margarine
1 tablespoon chopped parsley
¼ teaspoon dill weed

1. Combine ingredients for each recipe in a separate foil packet, leaving the tops open.
2. Pour 1 cup water into cooker and place foil packets on rack in cooker.
3. Cover, set control at 10 and place over high heat until control jiggles. Reduce heat and cook 25 minutes (or cook at 15 for 20 minutes).
4. Remove from heat and let cool 5 minutes; then run cold water over the cooker to finish reducing pressure.

Serves 2 (2½- or 4-quart cooker).
For a 6- or 8-quart cooker, use 1½ cups water in Step 2.

tip

The flavors of foods that are pressure-cooked together retain their own identities — they don't mix together. Thus, the foil packets are only used to keep the individual courses separate — to keep the sauce on the meat or to keep the potatoes out of the candied apples. The packets also simplify the job of removing the different courses from the cooker.

Pork Chops
Potatoes and Onions
Candied Apple Slices

Pork Chops

2 loin pork chops, ½ inch thick
2 tablespoons Worcestershire sauce
1 teaspoon Dijon mustard

Potatoes and Onions

2 baking potatoes, peeled and sliced paper-thin
½ onion, sliced paper-thin
1 tablespoon butter or margarine
  Pinch each of paprika, salt and pepper

Candied Apple Slices

1 large baking apple
2 tablespoons sugar
1 tablespoon butter or margarine

1. Sprinkle pork chops with Worcestershire sauce and then spread with mustard. Wrap in a foil packet, leaving the top open.
2. Layer potatoes and onion on a 12-inch square of foil, dotting each layer with butter. Sprinkle with paprika, salt and pepper. Shape foil into a packet, leaving the top open.
3. Core apple and cut into wedges. Place on a 12-inch square of foil. Sprinkle with sugar and dot with butter. Shape foil into a packet, leaving the top open.
4. Pour 1 cup water into cooker. Place packets of chops and potatoes on rack; place apple packet on top.
5. Cover, set control at 10 and cook over high heat until control jiggles. Reduce heat and cook 15 minutes (or cook at 15 for 12 minutes).
6. Run cold water over the cooker to reduce pressure instantly.

Serves 2 (2½-or 4-quart cooker).
For a 6- or 8-quart cooker, use 1½ cups water in Step 4. For a single meal, cut meat and vegetable recipes in half.

Rock Cornish Hens
Acorn Squash

Rock Cornish Hens

2 Rock Cornish hens (about 1 pound each)
4 tablespoons flour
2 tablespoons butter or margarine, softened
1 teaspoon paprika
½ teaspoon sage
¼ teaspoon pepper
2 tablespoons soy sauce

Acorn Squash

1 acorn squash
2 teaspoons brown sugar
2 teaspoons butter or margarine
¼ teaspoon salt
¼ teaspoon pepper

1. Place each bird on separate sheet of foil and dust with flour. Combine butter, paprika, sage, pepper and soy sauce to make a smooth paste and spread evenly over hens. Shape foil into packets, leaving the tops open.
2. Pour 1½ cups water into cooker and place packets on rack in cooker.
3. Cut squash in half, scoop out and discard seeds and pith, and place each half on a 12-inch square of foil.
4. Fill hollows of squash with brown sugar, butter, salt and pepper. Shape foil into packets, leaving the tops open. Place packets on rack, hollow side up, next to or on top of Rock Cornish hens.
5. Cover, set control at 10 and place over high heat until control jiggles. Reduce heat and cook 15 minutes (or cook at 15 for 13 minutes).
6. Remove from heat and let cool 5 minutes; then run cold water over the cooker to finish reducing pressure.
7. If desired, brown cooked hens under the broiler for a minute or two.

Serves 2 (6- or 8-quart cooker).
For a 2½- or 4-quart cooker, cut each recipe in half (or prepare the whole squash, if you wish); use 1 cup water in Step 2.

Fish Turbans
Zucchini and Walnuts
Tomatoes Fondue

Fish Turbans

2 large sole fillets (about 6 ounces
    each)
  Juice of ½ lemon
  Pinch each of salt and pepper
1 cup soft bread crumbs
¼ cup butter or margarine, melted
1 egg
2 tablespoons chopped parsley
1 clove garlic, minced
½ teaspoon each thyme and
    tarragon

Zucchini and Walnuts

1 medium zucchini
3 tablespoons butter or margarine,
    melted
¼ cup chopped toasted walnuts
1 teaspoon dill weed
  Pinch each of salt and pepper

Tomatoes Fondue

2 small ripe tomatoes, peeled,
    seeded and coarsely chopped
1 clove garlic, minced
¼ cup minced onion
1 tablespoon butter or margarine
  Pinch each of salt and pepper

1. Lay sole fillets flat on a 12-inch square of foil. Season both sides with lemon juice, salt and pepper.
2. Combine remaining ingredients for turbans; spoon onto sole fillets and roll up jelly-roll fashion to form turbans. Secure with wooden picks. Shape foil into a packet, leaving the top open.
3. Wash zucchini and cut into ½-inch slices; toss with butter. Combine walnuts, dill weed, salt and pepper; toss with zucchini until walnuts coat zucchini evenly. Wrap in a foil packet, leaving the top open.
4. On a 12-inch square of foil, combine the ingredients for Tomatoes Fondue. Shape foil into a packet, leaving the top open.
5. Pour 1½ cups water into cooker. Place foil packets on rack in cooker.

6. Cover, set control at 10 and place over high heat until control jiggles. Reduce heat and cook 8 minutes (or cook at 15 for 5 minutes).
7. Run cold water over the cooker to reduce pressure instantly.

Serves 2 (6- or 8-quart cooker).
For a 2½- or 4-quart cooker, make a single meal; cut each recipe in half and use 1 cup water in Step 5.

Turkey Wing
"Roasted" Yam
Kale

Turkey Wing

1 turkey wing
1 teaspoon butter or margarine
2 tablespoons barbecue sauce

"Roasted" Yam

1 yam

Kale

⅓ package (10½-ounce size) frozen
    kale
¼ teaspoon salt
1 tablespoon bacon-flavored bits

1. Place turkey wing on a 12-inch square of foil; dot with butter and pour on barbecue sauce. Shape foil into a packet, leaving the top open.
2. Wrap yam in a foil packet, leaving the top open.
3. Place frozen kale on a 12-inch square of foil; add salt and bacon bits. Shape foil into a packet, leaving the top open.
4. Pour 1 cup water into cooker. Arrange packets on rack, placing kale packet on top of yam packet.
5. Cover, set control at 10 and place over high heat until control jiggles. Reduce heat and cook 18 minutes (or cook at 15 for 15 minutes).
6. Run cold water over the cooker to reduce pressure instantly.

Serves 1 (2½- or 4-quart cooker).
For a 6- or 8-quart cooker, use 1½ cups water in Step 4.

tip

Frozen prepared main dishes can be reheated in no time in a pressure cooker. If the food is packaged in a foil dish, slit the foil on top and place on rack in cooker. (If packaged otherwise, unwrap and transfer to a foil packet, leaving top open.) Pour in 1 cup water for a 2½- or 4-quart cooker, 1½ cups water for a 6- or 8-quart cooker. Cover, set control at 15 and place over high heat. When control jiggles, reduce heat and cook for one-third the time suggested on the package. Run cold water over the cooker to reduce pressure instantly. (Note: do not use this method for fried foods.)

Chicken Teriyaki
Yellow Rice
Ginger Celery

Chicken Teriyaki

2 chicken breasts, boned and cut into strips
¼ cup orange juice
2 tablespoons soy sauce
1 tablespoon dry sherry
2 cloves garlic, minced
1 teaspoon brown sugar
¼ teaspoon ground ginger
　 Pinch each of cayenne pepper and dry mustard

Yellow Rice

¾ cup regular rice
1½ cups chicken stock or bouillon
　 Pinch of saffron or turmeric
1 teaspoon salt
¼ teaspoon pepper

Ginger Celery

3 stalks celery, cut into 3-inch pieces
1 tablespoon honey
　 Juice of ½ lemon
¼ teaspoon ground ginger
　 Pinch each of salt and pepper

1. Center chicken pieces on a 12-inch square of foil. Sprinkle with orange juice, soy sauce, sherry, garlic, brown sugar, ginger, cayenne pepper and mustard. Shape foil into a packet, leaving the top open.
2. Stir rice, stock, saffron, salt and pepper in a 1-quart heatproof bowl.
3. Place ingredients for Ginger Celery on a 12-inch square of foil. Shape into a packet, leaving the top open.
4. Pour 1 cup water into cooker. Place bowl of rice on rack. Place other packets on top of rice or alongside bowl.
5. Cover, set control at 10 and place over high heat until control jiggles. Reduce heat and cook 15 minutes (or cook at 15 for 12 minutes).
6. Remove from heat and let cool 5 minutes; then run cold water over the cooker to finish reducing pressure.

Serves 2 (2½- to 8-quart cooker).

STOCKS AND SOUPS —
IN SHORT ORDER

When you prepare a pot of stock — be it beef, chicken, turkey, fish or vegetable — you're making an excellent cooking investment. You reap an immediate return in terms of a hearty broth you can serve at once, plus a long-term dividend that can be stored for now, then used in many good meals to come — in main dishes, stews and sauces that will be all the more flavorful because they have been seasoned with the homemade stock. And now the process that traditionally took hours of simmering and left a stockpot well encrusted can be handled in mere minutes, with better extraction of flavor and far easier clean-up.

Borscht, Potato and Turnip Soup, Pistou and other hearty soups all profit from the pressure cooker treatment. It makes quick work of slow-to-soften ingredients, preserves the flavors and nutrients of vegetables and maximizes the contributions of bones and trimmings.

Even if it had no other uses, the pressure cooker would be worth its space as a soup and stock maker alone. The following recipes will attest to that.

Beef Stock

3 to 4 pounds meaty beef shin
    bones
4 medium carrots, cut into thick
    rounds
4 stalks celery, cut into thick slices
2 leeks, thoroughly washed and cut
    in half lengthwise
2 white turnips, peeled and cubed
2 quarts water
1 small bunch parsley
1 bay leaf
6 peppercorns
1 teaspoon thyme
1 teaspoon salt
1 teaspoon sugar

1. Place beef bones, carrots, celery,
leeks and turnips in cooker.
2. Add remaining ingredients.
3. Cover, set control at 15 and place
over high heat until control jiggles.
Reduce heat and cook 35 minutes.
4. Remove from heat and let cool 5
minutes; then run cold water over the
cooker to finish reducing pressure.
5. Strain stock through a fine sieve.
Reserve the meat and vegetables for a
hearty soup. Cover the stock and
refrigerate. (Stock will keep about 1
week in the refrigerator, 4 to 6 months in
the freezer.) Before using, discard fat
that will have solidified on the surface.

**Makes 2½ to 3 quarts (6- to 8-quart
cooker).**
Be sure the cooker is no more than ¾
full. For a 2½- or 4-quart cooker, cut the
recipe in half.

NOTE:
If time permits, before making the stock
cook bones, carrots, celery, leeks and
turnips in the cooker over moderate
heat, stirring occasionally, until the meat
and vegetables are evenly browned.
The process will take about 15 minutes
and contribute a deep, rich color to the
finished stock. (But the flavor will be
good whether or not you brown the
ingredients.)

Chicken Stock

3 pounds chicken necks, backs and
    wings (or whole chicken, cut up)
2 quarts cold water
1 bay leaf
6 peppercorns
4 cloves
1 teaspoon thyme
1 small bunch parsley
1 medium onion, coarsely chopped
1 medium carrot, diced
3 stalks celery, chopped
2 teaspoons salt

1. Rinse chicken under hot running
water until the water runs clear.
(Thorough rinsing prevents the finished
stock from becoming cloudy.)
2. Combine chicken and remaining
ingredients in cooker.
3. Cover, set control at 15 and place
over high heat until control jiggles.
Reduce heat and cook 35 minutes.
4. Remove from heat and let cool 5
minutes; then run cold water over the
cooker to finish reducing pressure.
5. Strain stock through a fine sieve.
Cover and refrigerate. (Stock will keep
about 1 week in the refrigerator, 4 to 6
months in the freezer.) Before using,
discard fat that will have solidified on the
surface.

2 to 2½ quarts (4- to 8-quart cooker).
Be sure the cooker is no more than ¾
full. For a 2½-quart cooker, cut the
recipe in half.

Turkey Stock

1 turkey carcass, cut into pieces
   (from a bird at least 12 pounds)
1 medium onion, chopped
1 medium carrot, chopped
4 stalks celery, chopped
2 cloves garlic, peeled
1 small bunch parsley
1 bay leaf
6 peppercorns
2 cloves
1 teaspoon each thyme and
   marjoram
  Pinch of sugar
2 quarts water

1. Combine all ingredients in cooker.
2. Cover, set control at 15 and place over high heat until control jiggles. Reduce heat and cook 30 minutes.
3. Remove from heat and let cool 5 minutes; then run cold water over the cooker to finish reducing pressure.
4. Strain stock through a fine sieve. Cover and refrigerate. (Stock will keep about 1 week in the refrigerator, 4 to 6 months in the freezer.) Before using, discard fat that will have solidified on the surface.

2 to 2½ quarts (4- to 8-quart cooker). Be sure the cooker is no more than ¾ full.

Fish Stock

1 medium onion, chopped
1 medium carrot, chopped
2 stalks celery, chopped
1 clove garlic, peeled
4 tablespoons butter or margarine
6 peppercorns
1 bay leaf
4 cloves
  Pinch each of thyme and tarragon
1 small bunch parsley stems
½ lemon, with peel
1 cup dry white wine
4 cups cold water
1½ pounds well-washed fish bones,
   heads and trimmings

1. Sauté onion, carrot, celery and garlic in butter in cooker, stirring, until vegetables are just tender.
2. Add remaining ingredients.
3. Cover, set control at 15 and place over high heat until control jiggles. Reduce heat and cook 7 minutes.
4. Remove from heat and let cool 5 minutes; then run cold water over the cooker to finish reducing pressure.
5. Strain stock through a fine sieve. Cover and refrigerate. (Stock will keep about 3 days in the refrigerator, 4 to 6 months in the freezer.) Before using, discard fat that will have solidified on the surface.

1¾ to 2 quarts (4- to 8-quart cooker). Be sure the cooker is no more than ¾ full. For a 2½-quart cooker, cut the recipe in half.

NOTE:
Use firm-fleshed, non-oily fish, such as sole or snapper, and do not overcook. (A fish stock, unlike other stocks, will turn bitter if it cooks too long.) And be sure to use only the stems of parsley. If you use the leafy tops, the stock will turn a muddy color.

tip

Meat, poultry and fish stocks should be cooled quickly to prevent spoilage. Chill, uncovered, in the refrigerator; then cover and store.

Vegetable Broth

¼ cup oil
2 cups each diced celery and
   onions
½ cup each diced carrots, turnips
   and tomatoes
½ cup mushrooms
   Pinch each of sugar and salt
6 peppercorns
1 bay leaf
1 small bunch parsley
1 teaspoon thyme
2 cloves garlic, peeled
2 quarts cold water

1. Heat oil in cooker. Sauté celery,
onions, carrots, turnips, tomatoes and
mushrooms, stirring constantly, until
onions are translucent.
2. Add remaining ingredients.
3. Cover, set control at 15 and place
over high heat until control jiggles.
Reduce heat and cook 25 minutes.
4. Remove from heat and let cool 5
minutes; then run cold water over the
cooker to finish reducing pressure.
5. Strain stock through a fine sieve.
Cover and refrigerate. (Stock will keep
about 1 week in the refrigerator, 4 to 6
months in the freezer.) Before using,
discard fat that will have solidified on the
surface.

2 to 2½ quarts (4- to 8-quart cooker).
Be sure the cooker is no more than ¾
full. For a 2½-quart cooker, cut the
recipe in half.

To Clarify Stock

2 quarts stock
4 egg whites and shells
1 stalk celery, minced
1 carrot, minced

1. In cooker, heat stock until simmering.
2. Beat egg whites, shells, celery and
carrot until frothy; beat into simmering
stock.
3. Cover, set control at 15 and place
over high heat until control jiggles.
Reduce heat and cook 1 minute.
4. Remove from heat and cool 5
minutes; then run cold water over the
cooker to finish reducing pressure.
5. Strain clarified stock through a double
layer of cheesecloth that has been
wrung out in cold water. Cover and
refrigerate.

(4- to 8-quart cooker).
For a 2½-quart cooker, cut the recipe in
half.

"Garbage" Soup

1 pound or more leftover cooked
   meat or poultry, with bones
2 cups or more assorted vegetables,
   cooked or raw
1 cup cooked potatoes, rice or pasta
1½ quarts water

1. Combine meat, vegetables and water
in cooker. (Remember, do not fill cooker
more than ¾ full.)
2. Cover, set control at 15 and place over
high heat until control jiggles. Reduce
heat and cook 10 minutes.
3. Remove from heat and let cool 5
minutes; then run cold water over the
cooker to finish reducing pressure.
4. Discard bones. Dice meat or poultry
and reserve. Whirl soup in blender or
puree in a food mill to make smooth.
5. Add the diced meat and reheat.
Season to taste with salt and pepper.

Serves 8 to 10 (6- or 8-quart cooker).
For a 2½- or 4-quart cooker, cut the
recipe in half.

tip

Many famous classic soups
originated as "garbage"
soup — they were made
with bits and pieces of
leftover meat and
vegetables that might
otherwise have been
discarded. Use your
leftovers — and your
imagination — to create
your own masterpiece.

Vegetable and Meat Soup

¼ cup oil
1 pound stew beef, cut into ½-inch cubes
1 baking potato, peeled and cut into ¾-inch cubes
2 small white turnips, peeled and cut into ¾-inch cubes
1 Spanish onion, coarsely chopped
2 medium carrots, peeled and cut into ¾-inch cubes
4 stalks celery, cut into thick slices
2 cups canned tomatoes, coarsely chopped, including liquid
1 cup dry red wine
1½ quarts beef stock or bouillon
1 teaspoon each marjoram, thyme and minced garlic
1 teaspoon salt
¼ teaspoon pepper
  Pinch of sugar

1. Heat oil in cooker; brown beef. Add remaining ingredients.
2. Cover, set control at 15 and place over high heat until control jiggles. Reduce heat and cook 10 minutes.
3. Remove from heat and let cool 5 minutes; then run cold water over the cooker to finish reducing pressure.
4. Garnish with croutons if desired.

Serves 6 to 8 (6- or 8-quart cooker).
For a 2½- or 4-quart cooker, cut the recipe in half.

NOTE:
Browning the meat first adds more meat flavor to the soup — and it also enhances the flavor of the meat itself.

Russian Sweet-Sour Cabbage Soup

¼ cup oil
4 tablespoons butter or margarine
1 Spanish onion, thinly sliced
4 cups each grated red and white cabbage
2 cloves garlic, minced
½ cup seedless raisins
½ cup dark brown sugar
1 teaspoon caraway seed
2 quarts chicken stock or bouillon
1 cup dry white wine
¼ cup cider vinegar

1. Heat oil and butter in cooker just until butter foams. Add onion and cabbage and cook, stirring, until cabbage is wilted.
2. Add remaining ingredients.
3. Cover, set control at 15 and place over high heat until control jiggles. Reduce heat and cook 10 minutes.
4. Remove from heat and let cool 5 minutes; then run cold water over the cooker to finish reducing pressure. Serve garnished with dairy sour cream if desired.

Serves about 6 (8-quart cooker).
For a 4- or 6-quart cooker, cut the recipe in half.

Black Bean Soup

1½ **cups dried black beans**
¼ **cup butter or margarine**
1 **cup coarsely chopped onion**
1 **stalk celery, minced**
1 **cup chopped peeled tomatoes**
6 **cloves garlic, minced**
1½ **quarts vegetable stock, chicken
    stock or chicken bouillon**
½ **cup dry sherry or Madeira**
1 **tablespoon chili powder**
1 **teaspoon grated orange peel**
1 **teaspoon sugar**

1. Par-cook, soak and drain black beans (page 26); reserve. Heat butter in cooker. Add onion and celery; cook, stirring frequently, until onion is translucent. Add beans and remaining ingredients.
2. Cover, set control at 15 and place over high heat until control jiggles. Reduce heat and cook 15 minutes.
3. Remove from heat and let cool 5 minutes; then run cold water over the cooker to finish reducing pressure.
4. Puree soup in a blender or food mill.
5. Garnish, if desired, with chopped hard-cooked egg and onion.

Serves 6 (6- or 8-quart cooker).
For a 2½- or 4-quart cooker, cut the recipe in half.

Matzoh Ball Soup

Matzoh Balls (right)
1 **stewing chicken (4 pounds), cut
    into 10 pieces**
2 **quarts water**
1 **bay leaf**
1 **teaspoon salt**
¼ **teaspoon pepper**
2 **carrots, cut into rounds**
1 **onion, minced**
4 **stalks celery, chopped**
2 **cloves garlic, minced**
1 **cup dry white wine**

1. Prepare Matzoh Balls.
2. Combine chicken, water, bay leaf, salt and pepper in cooker.

3. Cover, set control at 15 and place over high heat until control jiggles. Reduce heat and cook 20 minutes.
4. Remove from heat and let cool 5 minutes; then run cold water over the cooker to finish reducing pressure.
5. Cool slightly, then remove chicken meat from the bones. Discard the bones.
6. To the stock, add chicken meat, carrots, onion, celery, garlic and wine. Bring to the simmering point.
7. Moisten hands and shape matzoh ball mixture into dumplings about 1 inch in diameter; drop into simmering stock.
8. Cover, set control at 5 and place over high heat until control jiggles. Reduce heat and cook 8 minutes. (Or do not set control; cook with steam flowing from vent tube for 10 minutes.)
9. Remove from heat and let cool 5 minutes; then run cold water over the cooker to finish reducing pressure.

Serves 6 (8-quart cooker).
For a 4- or 6-quart cooker, cut the recipe in half, using 2 pounds chicken parts.

Matzoh Balls

3 **eggs, separated**
2 **tablespoons chicken fat,
    butter or margarine, melted**
1 **teaspoon salt**
4 **tablespoons water**
¾ **cup matzoh meal or cracker crumbs**

Beat egg yolks until light. Add fat, salt, water and matzoh meal. Beat egg whites until stiff and fold in. Cover and chill 1 hour or longer.

Meatball Soup

1 pound ground beef
¾ pound ground ham or pork
1 cup bread crumbs
2 cloves garlic, minced
2 eggs, beaten
¼ cup oil
1 cup each coarsely chopped onion,
    zucchini and celery
1 quart tomato juice
4 cups beef stock or bouillon
¼ cup grated Parmesan cheese
1 teaspoon dried dill weed or
    1 tablespoon fresh
1 tablespoon butter or margarine,
    softened
1 tablespoon flour

1. Combine beef, ham, bread crumbs, garlic and eggs; mix well. Form into ¾-inch balls.
2. Heat oil in cooker and brown meatballs a few at a time; remove and drain meatballs.
3. Add onion, zucchini and celery to the cooker and cook, stirring, until onion is translucent.
4. Add tomato juice, beef stock, cheese, dill and browned meatballs. Bring to a boil.
5. Blend butter and flour into a smooth paste. Stir into cooker.
6. Cover, set control at 15 and place over high heat until control jiggles. Reduce heat and cook 8 minutes.
7. Remove from heat and let cool 5 minutes; then run cold water over the cooker to finish reducing pressure.
8. Season to taste with salt and pepper. Ladle meatballs and vegetables into hot serving dishes and top with hot broth.

Serves 6 (6- or 8-quart cooker).
For a 2½- or 4-quart cooker, cut the recipe in half.

Borscht with Meat

1 pound lean beef, cut into ¾-inch
    cubes
4 beets, peeled and grated
3 carrots, grated
1 large Spanish onion, coarsely
    chopped
2 stalks celery, diced
2½ quarts beef or chicken stock
2 cloves garlic, minced
¼ teaspoon pepper
1 bay leaf
    Juice of 1 lemon
1 teaspoon sugar
    Dairy sour cream

1. Combine beef, beets, carrots, onion, celery, stock, garlic, pepper and bay leaf in cooker.
2. Cover, set control at 15 and place over high heat until control jiggles. Reduce heat and cook 25 minutes.
3. Remove from heat and let cool 5 minutes; then run cold water over the cooker to finish reducing pressure.
4. Stir in lemon juice and sugar. Season to taste with salt and pepper. Garnish with sour cream.

Serves 8 (6- or 8-quart cooker).
For a 2½- or 4-quart cooker, cut the recipe in half.

Potato and Turnip Soup

¼ cup butter or margarine
1 Spanish onion, minced
2 cups cubed peeled white turnips
2 cups cubed peeled potatoes
1 clove garlic, minced
½ teaspoon curry powder
2 teaspoons salt
¼ teaspoon white pepper
    Pinch of cinnamon
1 quart chicken stock or bouillon
¼ cup cooked rice
1 egg yolk, beaten
2 cups light cream
1 tablespoon chopped fresh dill or
    parsley

1. Melt butter in cooker. Add onion, turnips, potatoes and garlic; cook, stirring, until onion is translucent.
2. Add curry powder and cook, stirring constantly, 2 minutes, being careful not to burn the spice.
3. Add salt, pepper, cinnamon, stock and rice.
4. Cover, set control at 15 and place over high heat until control jiggles. Reduce heat and cook 12 minutes.
5. Remove from heat and let cool 5 minutes; then run cold water over the cooker to finish reducing pressure.
6. Warm egg yolk by adding a little hot soup to it and then add mixture to soup. Add cream and heat, uncovered, without boiling. Serve garnished with chopped dill.

Serves 6 (6- or 8-quart cooker).
For a 2½- or 4-quart cooker, cut the recipe in half.

Cock-A-Leekie

6 leeks
3 cups water
2 tablespoons chicken fat, butter or
    margarine
2 cups chicken stock or bouillon
1½ cups heavy cream
1 teaspoon salt
¼ teaspoon white pepper
¼ teaspoon sugar

1. Trim the green leafy tops off the leeks; shred enough of the tops to make about 2 tablespoons for garnish. Cut the white bulbous ends in half lengthwise and wash well under cold running water. Cut crosswise into thin slices (you should have about 4 cups).
2. Place leeks, water, chicken fat and chicken stock in cooker.
3. Cover, set control at 15 and place over high heat until control jiggles. Reduce heat and cook 15 minutes.
4. Run cold water over the cooker to reduce pressure instantly.
5. Stir in heavy cream and season with salt, pepper and sugar. Serve hot or cold, garnished with a sprinkling of the leek tops.

Serves 6 to 8 (2½- to 8-quart cooker).

New York Clam Chowder

4 tablespoons butter or margarine
4 slices bacon, cut into pieces
1 Spanish onion, minced
2 baking potatoes, peeled and diced
2 green peppers, seeded and
   chopped
4 stalks celery, chopped
2 cloves garlic, minced
1 quart clam broth or fish stock
½ cup dry white wine
2 cups canned, peeled tomatoes,
   chopped
1 teaspoon oregano
½ teaspoon thyme
2 cups minced clams (fresh or
   canned)

1. Melt butter in cooker. Add bacon, onion, potatoes, peppers, celery and garlic; cook, stirring, until onion is translucent.
2. Add clam broth, wine, tomatoes, oregano and thyme.
3. Cover, set control at 15 and place over high heat until control jiggles. Reduce heat and cook 7 minutes.
4. Remove from heat and let cool 5 minutes; then run cold water over the cooker to finish reducing pressure.
5. Stir in clams and heat through. Season to taste with salt and pepper. Serve with oyster crackers if desired.

Serves 6 (6- or 8-quart cooker).
For a 2½- or 4-quart cooker, cut the recipe in half.

New England Clam Chowder

3 to 4 ounces salt pork or 6 slices
   bacon, diced
4 stalks celery, chopped
2 large potatoes, peeled and diced
1 Spanish onion, chopped
1 quart clam broth or fish stock
½ teaspoon thyme
2 cups minced clams (fresh or
   canned)
3 cups milk or light cream
6 or more soda crackers, crumbled

1. Render salt pork in cooker. Add celery, potatoes and onion; cook, stirring, until onion is translucent.
2. Add clam broth and thyme to cooker.
3. Cover, set control at 15 and place over high heat until control jiggles. Reduce heat and cook 4 minutes.
4. Run cold water over the cooker to reduce pressure instantly.
5. Stir in minced clams, milk and crumbled soda crackers. Cook, stirring, over moderate heat until thickened. Season to taste with salt and white pepper. Serve with oyster crackers if desired.

Serves 6 (6- or 8-quart cooker).
For a 2½- or 4-quart cooker, cut the recipe in half.

Cioppino

½ cup olive oil
2 cloves garlic, minced
1 onion, coarsely chopped
1 green pepper, seeded and chopped
¼ cup chopped parsley
1 can (8 ounces) tomatoes, with
liquid
1 bay leaf
1 cup dry red wine
2 pounds striped bass fillets, cut into
1-inch cubes
1 large Dungeness crab or 1 pound
king crab legs
1 pint mussels or littleneck clams,
with liquid

1. Heat oil in cooker. Add garlic, onion, green pepper and parsley; cook, stirring, until onion is wilted. Add remaining ingredients.
2. Cover, set control at 10 and place over high heat until control jiggles. Reduce heat and cook 7 minutes (or cook at 15 for 5½ minutes).
3. Remove from heat and let cool 5 minutes; then run cold water over the cooker to finish reducing pressure.
4. Season to taste with salt and pepper. Spoon into heated soup bowls.

Serves 4 (2½- to 8-quart cooker).
This recipe can be doubled in a 6- or 8-quart cooker.

Soupe au Pistou

3 medium zucchini, washed and
grated
2 slices bacon, diced
½ cup olive oil
1½ cups coarsely chopped onions
4 cloves garlic, minced
1½ quarts boiling water
2 cups shelled fresh lima beans
¼ cup minced fresh basil
½ cup minced parsley
½ cup grated Parmesan cheese
1 teaspoon salt
¼ teaspoon pepper

1. Wrap zucchini in cheesecloth and squeeze out liquid. Reserve both liquid and zucchini.
2. Cook bacon, oil, onions and garlic in cooker over moderate heat, stirring, until onions are translucent.
3. Add zucchini and the remaining ingredients except the reserved zucchini liquid.
4. Cover, set control at 15 and place over high heat until control jiggles. Reduce heat and cook 15 minutes.
5. Remove from heat and let cool 5 minutes; then run cold water over the cooker to finish reducing pressure.
6. Stir in the reserved zucchini liquid (this will tint the soup a pleasant light green) and adjust seasoning to taste.

Serves 6 to 8 (6- or 8-quart cooker).
For a 2½- or 4-quart cooker, cut the recipe in half.

BEANS AND RICE AND PORRIDGE, TOO

So you thought Uncle Charlie's recipe for baked beans couldn't be beat. And that your neighbor's chili had no equal. Think again. For the following pages open up an easy new world of incomparable bean cookery — ranging from Cassoulet to Cuban Black Beans and Rice. Beans that cook in one to five minutes instead of close to an hour and soybeans that turn tender in 35 minutes instead of three hours set more than speed records. As energy costs go up, these savings serve to restore the economy of cooking beans. What's more, pressure-cooked beans have a silky texture and delicate flavor.

Rice and cereals, too, seem better than ever. Cooked under pressure they expand to a smooth fullness once associated only with long, slow cooking and constant stirring. Whether you're handling Spanish Rice or Super Steel Oats, the jiggling of the control indicates that the steam is doing the cooking smoothly and uniformly.

Dried Beans

To prepare dried beans for cooking, first par-cook and soak them.
• In a 2½-quart cooker, use no more than 2 cups dried beans.
• In a 4-quart cooker, use no more than 3 cups dried beans.
• In a 6-quart cooker, use no more than 6 cups dried beans.
• In an 8-quart cooker, use no more than 8 cups dried beans.
(Dried beans double in volume when fully cooked.)

To par-cook and soak:
1. Place beans in cooker. Add 2 cups water and 1 tablespoon oil for every 1 cup of dried beans.
2. Cover, set control at 15 and place over high heat until control jiggles. Remove from heat at once.
3. Let pressure reduce naturally.
4. Drain. Beans are now ready to cook, alone or in combination with other foods.

To cook:
1. Place par-cooked and soaked beans in cooker. Add ½ cup water and 1 tablespoon oil for every 1 cup of beans.
2. Cover, set control at 15 and place over high heat until control jiggles. Reduce heat and cook required length of time (see chart below).
3. Remove from heat and let cool 5 minutes; then run cold water over the cooker to finish reducing pressure.
4. Drain, if necessary.

Timetable for Cooking Par-Cooked and Soaked Beans

Type	Control Setting	Minutes to cook after control jiggles
Black Beans	15	5
Great Northern Beans	15	5
Kidney Beans	15	1
Lima Beans (large)	15	2
Lima Beans (small)	15	1½
Navy Pea Beans	15	3
Pink Beans	15	2½
Pinto Beans	15	5
Red Beans (small)	15	3
Roman Beans	15	3
Soy Beans	15	35

Black-Eyed Peas and Lentils

Par-cooking and soaking are not necessary for black-eyed peas and lentils. The maximum quantities that you can use in your cooker are the same as those for other Dried Beans (above).

To cook:
1. Place black-eyed peas or lentils in cooker. Add 2 cups water and 1 tablespoon oil for every 1 cup of dried beans.
2. Cover, set control at 15 and place over high heat until control jiggles. Reduce heat and cook 14 minutes.
3. Remove from heat and let cool 5 minutes; then run cold water over the cooker to finish reducing pressure.
4. Drain, if necessary.

Cassoulet

1 cup (about ½ pound) dried great
  northern beans
½ pound sweet Italian sausage,
  sliced
½ pound boneless fresh pork or
  lamb, cut into 1-inch cubes
2 cloves garlic, chopped
1 can (20 ounces) solid-pack
  tomatoes
  Bouquet garni (parsley, celery tops
  and bay leaf tied together)
1 onion, peeled and studded with 2
  cloves
½ teaspoon salt
¼ teaspoon pepper
½ cup buttered bread crumbs

1. Par-cook, soak and drain beans
(page 26); reserve.
2. Brown sausage and pork in cooker.
Add garlic and cook 1 minute longer.
3. Drain tomatoes and measure liquid.
Add water to make 1 cup liquid. Stir into
cooker with tomatoes, beans, bouquet
garni, cloved onion, salt and pepper.
4. Cover, set control at 15 and place
over high heat until control jiggles.
Reduce heat and cook 5 minutes.
5. Remove from heat and let cool 5
minutes; then run cold water over the
cooker to finish reducing pressure.
6. Discard bouquet garni and cloved
onion. Adjust seasoning to taste.
7. Transfer meat and beans to a
heatproof serving casserole and
sprinkle with bread crumbs. Brown
quickly under the broiler.

Serves 4 (2½- or 4-quart cooker).
For a 6- or 8-quart cooker, add enough
water to make 1½ cups liquid in Step 3.
Or double the recipe, using 2 cups liquid
in Step 3.

Boston Baked Beans

2 cups (about 1 pound) dried navy
  pea beans
¼ pound salt pork, sliced, or
  4 slices bacon
1 onion, chopped
¼ cup dark molasses
½ teaspoon dry mustard
¼ cup brown sugar
  Dash of Worcestershire sauce

1. Par-cook, soak and drain beans
(page 26), reserving 1 cup of cooking
liquid.
2. Return beans to cooker. Add salt pork
and reserved cooking liquid.
3. Cover, set control at 15 and place
over high heat until control jiggles.
Reduce heat and cook 3 minutes.
4. Remove from heat and let cool 5
minutes; then run cold water over the
cooker to finish reducing pressure.
5. Add onion, molasses, mustard, brown
sugar and Worcestershire sauce.
6. Cook over high heat until sauce is
thickened, stirring occasionally with a
fork. Season to taste with salt and
pepper.

Serves 6 (2½- to 8-quart cooker).
This recipe can be doubled in a 6- or
8-quart cooker; reserve 2 cups cooking
liquid in Step 1.

tip

It's not done enough?
Simply close your cooker
again (adding water if the
directions called for it) and
pressure-cook a few
minutes longer. Meats and
other foods — particularly
beans — vary widely in age,
consistency, moisture
content and shape, even
when the weights are the
same. And these variances
— as well as individual taste
preferences — affect
cooking times.

Prize-Winning Chili

1 cup (about ½ pound) dried red
    kidney beans or 1 can
    (16 ounces) red kidney beans
1 pound ground beef
1 clove garlic, chopped
1 medium onion, chopped
1 green pepper, chopped
1 can (4 ounces) green chili
    peppers, chopped
½ cup chopped parsley
1 teaspoon cumin
1 teaspoon oregano
1 teaspoon chili powder
½ teaspoon salt
¼ teaspoon pepper
1 can (16 ounces) tomatoes,
    broken up, with liquid
1 can (6 ounces) tomato paste
½ cup water
¼ cup dairy sour cream
2 teaspoons lime juice

1. Par-cook, soak and drain dried kidney
beans (page 26), or rinse well if using
canned beans; reserve.
2. Brown meat in cooker, stirring
continuously with a fork. Drain off
excess fat.
3. Add garlic, onion, green pepper, chili
peppers, parsley and seasonings. Cook
until onion is soft.
4. Stir in tomatoes, tomato paste, water
and kidney beans.
5. Cover, set control at 15 and place
over high heat until control jiggles.
Reduce heat and cook 10 minutes.
6. Remove from heat and let cool 5
minutes; then run cold water over the
cooker to finish reducing pressure.
7. Adjust seasoning to taste. Garnish
with a mixture of sour cream and lime
juice.

Serves 6 (4- to 8-quart cooker).

Southwestern Pintos

2 cups (about 1 pound) dried pinto
    beans
4 tablespoons bacon fat
1 onion, diced
2 cloves garlic, chopped
2 cups water
1 tablespoon minced parsley
1 can (8 ounces) prepared taco
    sauce

1. Par-cook, soak and drain beans
(page 26); reserve.
2. Heat bacon fat in cooker. Add onion
and garlic; cook until onion is
translucent. Add beans, water and
parsley.
3. Cover, set control at 15 and place
over high heat until control jiggles.
Reduce heat and cook 5 minutes.
4. Remove from heat and let cool 5
minutes; then run cold water over the
cooker to finish reducing pressure.
5. Add taco sauce. Cook, uncovered,
over high heat until sauce is thickened.
6. Season to taste with salt, pepper and
hot pepper sauce.

Serves 6 (2½- to 8-quart cooker).
This recipe can be doubled in a 6- or
8-quart cooker.

Soy Beans, Spanish Style

2 cups (about 1 pound) dried soy
    beans
1 teaspoon shortening
¼ cup chopped onion
¼ cup diced green pepper
1 can (16 ounces) tomatoes, broken
    up, with liquid
1½ teaspoons salt
½ teaspoon basil
¼ teaspoon chili powder
¼ teaspoon pepper
2 slices soft white bread, crumbled
¾ cup grated sharp cheddar cheese

1. Par-cook, soak and drain soy beans
(page 26); reserve.
2. Melt shortening in 1½-quart
heatproof casserole. Sauté onion and
green pepper until onion is translucent.
3. Add tomatoes, seasonings and bread;
mix well. Stir in beans. Top with cheese.
4. Pour 1 cup water into cooker.
Place casserole on rack in cooker.
5. Cover, set control at 15 and place
over high heat until control jiggles.
Reduce heat and cook 50 minutes.
6. Remove from heat and let cool 5
minutes; then run cold water over the
cooker to finish reducing pressure.

Serves 4 to 6 (6- or 8-quart cooker).
A 2½- or 4-quart cooker can be used if
your casserole fits.

Beans with Beef

1 cup dried kidney beans or small
    lima beans
1 pound ground beef
2 onions, sliced
1 can (16 ounces) solid-pack
    tomatoes
½ teaspoon salt
    Pinch of pepper
    Dash of Worcestershire sauce

1. Par-cook, soak and drain beans (page
26); reserve.

2. Heat cooker slightly. Add beef and
cook, stirring, until beef loses its red
color.
3. Add onions and cook, stirring, until
onions are translucent.
4. Drain tomatoes and measure liquid. If
necessary, add water to make ⅔ cup
liquid. Add tomato liquid, tomatoes,
beans and seasonings to cooker.
5. Cover, set control at 15 and place over
high heat until control jiggles. Reduce
heat and cook 2 minutes.
6. Run cold water over the cooker to
reduce pressure instantly.

Serves 4 (2½- or 4-quart cooker).
For a 6- or 8-quart cooker, add enough
water to make 1⅓ cups liquid in Step 4.

Cuban Black Beans and Rice

1 cup (about ½ pound) dried black
    beans
3 tablespoons butter or margarine
1 onion, chopped
2 cloves garlic, chopped
1 cup rice
2 cups water
1 teaspoon salt
¼ teaspoon pepper

1. Par-cook, soak and drain beans
(page 26); reserve.
2. Melt butter in cooker. Add onion
and cook, stirring, until translucent.
3. Add garlic and rice and cook, stirring,
until rice is golden.
4. Remove from heat and let cool 5
minutes. Add water and beans.
5. Cover, set control at 15 and place
over high heat until control jiggles.
Reduce heat and cook 5 minutes.
6. Remove from heat and let cool 5
minutes; then run cold water over the
cooker to finish reducing pressure.
7. Season with salt and pepper.

Serves 4 (2½- to 8-quart cooker).
This recipe can be doubled in a 6- or
8-quart cooker.

menu idea

Guacamole Dip

*Cuban Black Beans and Rice
(this page)*

Corn Sticks

Flan (p. 106)   *Cuban Coffee*

Fluffy Rice

1. Fill the cooker half full of water and bring to a boil. Add rice (1 cup regular rice makes 3 cups cooked) and butter or margarine (½ tablespoon for every 1 cup of rice):
• For a 2½-quart cooker, use no more than 1 cup rice.
• For a 4-quart cooker, use no more than 2 cups rice.
• For a 6-quart cooker, use no more than 4 cups rice.
• For an 8-quart cooker, use no more than 6 cups rice.
(The cooker should always be half full of water, even if you use less than the maximum amount of rice.)
2. Cover, set control at 15 and place over *moderate* heat until control jiggles. Reduce heat and cook 7 minutes for firm grains, 8 minutes for softer grains.
3. Run cold water over the cooker to reduce pressure instantly.
4. Drain rice. Grains will be tender and separate, not starchy or gummy.

Converted Rice

Increase cooking time to 10 minutes.

Brown Rice

Increase cooking time to 22 minutes.

Spanish Rice

3 cups cooked rice (above)
2 tablespoons butter or margarine
2 large onions, sliced
1 large green pepper, sliced
1 can (16 ounces) solid-pack
   tomatoes
1 tablespoon sugar
2 teaspoons salt
¼ teaspoon pepper

1. Cook rice as directed.
2. Melt butter in cooker; add onions and green pepper and cook until onions are soft. Add tomatoes and seasonings.
3. Cover, set control at 15 and place over *moderate* heat until control jiggles. Reduce heat and cook 4 minutes.
4. Run cold water over the cooker to reduce pressure instantly.
5. Stir cooked rice into cooker and heat through.

Serves 6 (2½- to 8-quart cooker).

NOTE:
For a quick luncheon or main dish for four, add cooked sausages, meat or chicken to Spanish Rice.

Risotto

2 tablespoons butter or margarine
2 small onions, finely chopped
1 cup regular rice
½ teaspoon salt
   Pinch of white pepper
1 cup white wine
1¼ cups chicken stock or bouillon
¼ cup grated Parmesan cheese

1. Melt butter in a saucepan. Add onions and cook until translucent but not browned. Add rice, salt and pepper; cook, stirring, 2 minutes. Transfer rice mixture to a 1-quart heatproof mold.
2. Stir in wine and stock.
3. Pour 1½ cups water into cooker. Place mold on rack in cooker.
4. Cover, set control at 5 and place over high heat until control jiggles. Reduce heat and cook 15 minutes (or cook at 15 for 12 minutes).
5. Run cold water over the cooker to reduce pressure instantly.
6. Stir in cheese and, if desired, more butter.

Serves 4 to 6 (2½- to 8-quart cooker).

NOTE:
To make Risotto Milanese, soak a pinch of saffron threads in the chicken stock before adding it to the rice.

Cornmeal Mush

4 cups water
1 cup yellow cornmeal
1 tablespoon butter or margarine
1 teaspoon salt

1. Mix 1 cup water with cornmeal to make a paste.
2. Bring remaining water, butter and salt to a boil in cooker. Stir in cornmeal paste. Cook 2 minutes, stirring.
3. Cover, set control at 15 and place over *moderate* heat until control jiggles. Reduce heat and cook 10 minutes.
4. Remove from heat and let cool 5 minutes; then run cold water over the cooker to finish reducing pressure. Serve at once.
5. As a breakfast cereal, top with brown sugar or syrup; or, top with butter, salt and pepper and serve as an accompaniment for ham or other meats.

Serves 4 (4- to 8-quart cooker).
For a 2½-quart cooker, cut the recipe in half.

Scrapple

Cornmeal Mush (left)
½ pound pork sausage meat, crumbled
1 clove garlic, minced
1 tablespoon poultry seasoning

1. Prepare Cornmeal Mush as directed, but stir sausage meat, garlic and poultry seasoning into water with the cornmeal paste.
2. Cover, set control at 15 and place over *moderate* heat until control jiggles. Reduce heat and cook 10 minutes.
3. Remove from heat and let cool 5 minutes; then run cold water over the cooker to finish reducing pressure.
4. Season scrapple to taste with salt, pepper and cayenne.
5. Pour mixture into an 8½ x 4½ x 2½-inch loaf pan lined with foil. Chill thoroughly.
6. Just before serving, cut into slices and brown on both sides in hot bacon fat.

Serves 6 (4- to 8-quart cooker).

Gnocchi

Cornmeal Mush (above)
½ cup softened butter or margarine
1 cup grated Parmesan cheese
2 eggs, beaten

1. Prepare Cornmeal Mush. Beat half the butter and half the cheese into the mush. Beat in eggs.
2. Spread ⅓ inch thick in a buttered pan or platter. Chill.
3. Cut into diamonds or squares; transfer to a heatproof serving dish, overlapping pieces as necessary.
4. Sprinkle with remaining cheese and dot with remaining butter. Heat in 350°F oven until cheese is melted and lightly browned.

Serves 6 (4- to 8-quart cooker).

Grits

1 cup grits
3 cups cold water
1 teaspoon salt
2 tablespoons butter or margarine

1. Stir grits with cold water in cooker until smooth. Add salt and butter and bring to a boil. Stir until smooth.
2. Cover, set control at 15 and place over *moderate* heat until control jiggles. Reduce heat and cook 16 minutes.
3. Remove from heat and let cool 5 minutes; then run cold water over the cooker to finish reducing pressure.
4. Serve with sugar or syrup at breakfast, or as a substitute for potatoes or noodles at other meals.

Serves 4 (4- to 8-quart cooker).
For a 2½-quart cooker, cut the recipe in half.

tip

Grits are finely ground hominy, or samp, a cereal made of the kernels of dried corn, with hulls and germs removed. Both hominy and grits are favorites on Southern tables, but raw hominy is generally unavailable in other parts of the country. If you can find hominy, cook it as you would grits, but increase cooking time to 1 hour.

Cereal Blend

3⅓ cups water
  1 cup rolled oats
  ¼ cup farina
  ¼ cup whole wheat cereal
  1 teaspoon salt
  2 tablespoons butter or margarine

1. Bring water to a boil in cooker. Add cereals, salt and butter; stir until blended.
2. Cover, set control at 15 and place over *moderate* heat until control jiggles. Reduce heat and cook 5 minutes.
3. Remove from heat and let cool 5 minutes; then run cold water over the cooker to finish reducing pressure.

Serves 4 to 6 (4- to 8-quart cooker).
For a 2½-quart cooker, cut the recipe in half.

NOTE:
For breakfast variety, make your own cereal blends. Adjust the amount of water according to directions on the package, using an appropriate amount for each cereal. The Cereal Blend recipe, for instance, includes 2 cups water for the oats, ⅔ cup for the farina and ⅔ cup for the whole wheat cereal. Add 1 or 2 tablespoons butter or margarine to prevent frothing. Pressure-cook over *moderate* heat at 15 for the time required for the longest-cooking cereal. (Remember, for pressure-cooking, decrease the time recommended on the label by one-third.)

Mellow Old-Fashioned Oats

2 cups water
1 cup rolled oats
½ teaspoon salt
1 tablespoon butter or margarine

1. Bring water to a boil in cooker; stir in oats, salt and butter.
2. Cover, set control at 15 and place over *moderate* heat until control jiggles. Reduce heat and cook 5 minutes.
3. Remove from heat and let cool 5 minutes; then run cold water over the cooker to finish reducing pressure.

Serves 3 or 4 (4- to 8-quart cooker).
For a 2½-quart cooker, cut the recipe in half. This recipe can also be doubled in a 6- or 8-quart cooker.

Super Steel Oats

2½ cups water
  1 cup steel-cut oats
  ½ teaspoon salt
  2 tablespoons butter or margarine

1. Bring water to a boil in cooker; stir in oats, salt and butter.
2. Cover, set control at 15 and place over *moderate* heat until control jiggles. Reduce heat and cook 30 minutes.
3. Remove from heat and let cool 5 minutes; then run cold water over the cooker to finish reducing pressure.
4. Serve with more butter, brown sugar, and milk or cream.

Serves 3 or 4 (4- to 8-quart cooker).
For a 2½-quart cooker, cut the recipe in half. This recipe can also be doubled in a 6- or 8-quart cooker.

An elegant and easy dinner for two — Rock Cornish Hens and Acorn Squash (page 12).

Clockwise: Black Bean Soup (page 20), Borscht with Meat (page 21), Cock-A-Leekie (page 22).

The French have a way with beans, sausage and pork — they call it Cassoulet (page 27).

For family or for company — Lamb Curry (page 41) and an array of accompaniments.

INTERNATIONAL ENTRÉES

It's time for "something different." Perhaps company's coming and you want to make an impression. Or Johnny came home with straight A's and you feel a spur-of-the-moment celebration is in order. Or maybe you're just a bit bored with cooking — and eating — the same family favorites. Whatever the reason, you can add an extra-special spark to your mealtimes if you let your thoughts go wandering. And we do mean wandering.

Think about the whole wide world of taste adventures, and the special flair of foreign fare. You can bring back memories of last year's trip to Europe. Or duplicate the meal you had in that charming French restaurant. Or what about hosting a Spanish-style dinner party, with the table decorated to complement your menu?

On the following pages you'll find a delicious sampling of international specialties, all adapted to the speed and ease of the pressure cooker. Included are Boeuf Bourguignonne, tender cubes of beef in a hearty wine sauce . . . Paella Valenciana, delicate morsels of chicken and shrimp with golden saffron rice . . . Chicken Javanese, a whole chicken topped with an intriguing peanut butter–curry sauce . . . Chinese Spareribs . . . Swedish Fish Pudding . . . and many more. Any one of these is sure to add the just-right accent to your meal plans.

What's more, you'll discover that the pressure cooker, like jet travel, vastly reduces the time required for your worldwide adventures.

Chinese Beef and Peppers

1½ pounds thin-sliced round or flank
    steak
1½ tablespoons soy sauce
 ¼ cup sherry
  2 tablespoons oil
  2 bell peppers, cut into strips
  2 stalks celery, sliced diagonally
  1 onion, cut into thick slices
 ¾ cup beef bouillon or stock
1½ teaspoons cornstarch

1. Coat steak slices in mixture of soy and sherry.
2. Heat oil in cooker. Add meat and cook, stirring, until browned. Add peppers, celery, onion, bouillon and remaining soy-sherry mixture.
3. Cover, set control at 10 and place over high heat until control jiggles. Reduce heat and cook 6 minutes (or cook at 15 for 4 minutes).
4. Run cold water over the cooker to reduce pressure instantly.
5. Blend cornstarch with a little water to make a smooth paste. Add to cooker and heat, stirring, until thickened. Season to taste with salt and pepper and more soy sauce. Serve with rice.

Serves 4 (2½- to 8-quart cooker).

Steak and Kidney Stew

  2 beef kidneys
  1 tablespoon vinegar
  1 teaspoon salt
  1 pound round steak, cut into
    ¾-inch cubes
    Flour, salt and pepper
  6 small potatoes, peeled and
    quartered
  6 small carrots, scraped and
    quartered
  1 onion, chopped
  2 tablespoons chopped parsley
1½ cups boiling water

1. Prepare kidneys for cooking by removing fat, tubes and gristle. Reserve fat. Slice kidneys and cover with cold water; add vinegar and salt and soak 1 hour. Drain kidneys and pat dry.
2. Coat steak cubes with flour mixed with salt and pepper.
3. Rub bottom of cooker with reserved kidney fat. Add kidneys, steak, potatoes, carrots, onion, parsley and boiling water.
4. Cover, set control at 10 and place over high heat until control jiggles. Reduce heat and cook 18 minutes (or cook at 15 for 15 minutes).
5. Remove from heat and let cool 5 minutes; then run cold water over the cooker to finish reducing pressure.
6. Adjust seasoning to taste. Serve with rice or noodles.

Serves 6 (2½- to 8-quart cooker).
This recipe can be doubled in a 6- or 8-quart cooker.

NOTE:
This recipe can be made as a Steak and Kidney Pie if you like. Simply prepare the pastry for a one-crust pie. Turn the cooked stew into a pie plate or casserole and top with the rolled-out pastry. Cut a vent in the pastry to allow steam to escape. Bake in a hot (450° F) oven for 15 minutes, until crust is nicely browned.

tip

Reheating leftovers? Use your pressure cooker for casserole mixtures and creamed combinations. Here's a "stick-proof" method: Turn the food into a metal mold or ovenproof bowl and place on rack in cooker (with 1 cup water in cooker). Cover, set control at 15 and place over high heat. When control jiggles, remove from heat and let pressure drop naturally.

Rouladen
(Beef Birds)

2 pounds round steak, sliced ¼-inch
    thick
1 teaspoon salt
1 onion, chopped
2 cloves garlic, crushed
½ pound pork sausage
1½ cups soft whole wheat bread
    crumbs
1 teaspoon poultry seasoning
½ cup chopped parsley
½ teaspoon salt
    Pinch of pepper
    Beef bouillon or water to moisten
    (about 3 tablespoons)
¾ cup beef bouillon or red wine

1. Cut the steak slices into 8 rectangles. Pound between sheets of waxed paper to flatten slightly. Sprinkle with 1 teaspoon salt.
2. Cook onion, garlic and sausage in a skillet until browned. Pour off excess fat and reserve.
3. To the skillet add bread crumbs, poultry seasoning, chopped parsley, ½ teaspoon salt, pepper and enough bouillon to moisten.
4. Divide the stuffing onto the steak pieces. Roll up and secure with wooden picks.
5. Heat 2 tablespoons of the reserved sausage drippings in cooker; brown stuffed rolls on all sides. Add remaining ¾ cup bouillon.
6. Cover, set control at 10 and place over high heat until control jiggles. Reduce heat and cook 25 minutes (or cook at 15 for 20 minutes).
7. Remove from heat and let cool 5 minutes; then run cold water over the cooker to finish reducing pressure.
8. With fork, test rolls for tenderness. If necessary, pressure-cook 1 or 2 minutes longer. Remove rolls to serving casserole; discard picks.
9. If desired, boil pan gravy to thicken to desired consistency. Pour over beef birds in casserole.

Serves 8 (2½- or 4-quart cooker).
For a 6- or 8-quart cooker, use 1¼ cups bouillon or wine.

Boeuf Bourguignonne

2 pounds beef chuck, cut into 1-inch
    cubes
4 tablespoons butter or margarine
2 onions, chopped
1 teaspoon salt
½ teaspoon pepper
1½ cups dry red wine
1 bay leaf
6 to 8 whole carrots, scraped
12 to 16 small whole white onions,
    peeled
½ pound mushrooms
2 tablespoons butter or margarine,
    softened
2 tablespoons flour
    Chopped parsley

1. In cooker, brown beef cubes in butter. Remove to a bowl.
2. Sauté chopped onions in cooker until translucent. Return meat to cooker; add salt, pepper, wine and bay leaf.
3. Cover, set control at 10 and place over high heat until control jiggles. Reduce heat and cook 15 minutes (or cook at 15 for 12 minutes).
4. Remove from heat and let cool 5 minutes; then run cold water over the cooker to finish reducing pressure.
5. Open cooker; add carrots, onions and mushrooms.
6. Cover, set control at 10 and place over high heat until control jiggles. Reduce heat and cook 10 minutes (or cook at 15 for 6 minutes).
7. Run cold water over the cooker to reduce pressure instantly.
8. Blend butter and flour to make a smooth paste. Add to cooker bit by bit and cook, stirring, until sauce is thickened. Serve garnished with parsley.

Serves 6 (4- to 8-quart cooker).
For a 2½-quart cooker, cut the recipe in half. This recipe can also be doubled in an 8-quart cooker.

Blanquette de Veau
(French Veal Stew)

2 pounds boneless veal, cut into
    1-inch cubes
1 carrot
1 onion, peeled and studded with
    2 cloves
    Pinch of thyme
2 cups water
2 tablespoons butter or margarine
3 tablespoons flour
12 small whole white onions (cooked
    or canned)
½ pound mushroom caps
    Juice of ½ lemon
1 teaspoon salt
    Pinch of white pepper
2 egg yolks
½ cup light cream or half-and-half
    Chopped parsley

1. Place veal, carrot, cloved onion,
thyme and water in cooker; bring to a
boil and skim.
2. Cover, set control at 10 and place
over high heat until control jiggles.
Reduce heat and cook 12 minutes (or
cook at 15 for 10 minutes).
3. Run cold water over the cooker to
reduce pressure instantly.
4. Transfer meat to a heatproof serving
casserole. Strain stock through a fine
sieve; discard carrot and onion.
5. Melt butter In a saucepan; add flour
and cook for a minute, stirring, without
allowing the roux to brown. Add strained
stock and cook, stirring, until gravy is
thickened and smooth.
6. Add small onions, mushroom caps,
lemon juice, salt and pepper; heat
through. Add to veal in casserole.
7. Just before serving, reheat veal in
casserole if necessary. Beat egg yolks
lightly with cream; warm with a little hot
gravy and stir into casserole. Heat
without boiling. Garnish with parsley and
serve with buttered noodles.

Serves 6 (2½- to 8-quart cooker).
This recipe can be doubled in an 8-quart
cooker.

Veal Goulash

3 tablespoons butter or margarine
2 pounds boneless veal, cut into
    1-inch cubes
3 onions, thinly sliced
½ cup water
1 tablespoon paprika
1 can (16 ounces) tomatoes, with
    liquid
½ teaspoon caraway seed
1 teaspoon salt
¼ teaspoon pepper
1 can (8 ounces) sliced mushrooms
½ cup dairy sour cream

1. Melt butter in cooker. Add veal and
onions; cook over low heat, stirring
often, until veal cubes are browned.
2. Add water, paprika, tomatoes,
caraway seed, salt and pepper.
3. Cover, set control at 10 and place
over high heat until control jiggles.
Reduce heat and cook 20 minutes (or
cook at 15 for 16 minutes.)
4. Remove from heat and let cool 5
minutes; then run cold water over the
cooker to finish reducing pressure.
5. With a slotted spoon, transfer veal to
a heated serving dish; keep warm.
6. Drain mushrooms and add liquid to
sauce in cooker; if sauce seems too
thin, boil rapidly to thicken. Then reduce
heat; add mushrooms and sour cream
and heat through without boiling. Adjust
seasoning to taste. Pour over veal.

Serves 4 (2½- or 4-quart cooker).
For a 6- or 8-quart cooker, use 1 cup
water.

Chinese Spareribs

¼ cup oil
2 pounds spareribs, cut into
    individual portions
4 large cloves garlic, chopped
1½ cups water
2 tablespoons soy sauce
2 teaspoons sugar
½ teaspoon salt

1. Heat oil in cooker and brown
spareribs. Pour off excess fat.
2. Mix remaining ingredients and pour
over spareribs.
3. Cover, set control at 10 and place
over high heat until control jiggles.
Reduce heat and cook 15 minutes (or
cook at 15 for 12 minutes).
4. Remove from heat and let cool 5
minutes; then run cold water over the
cooker to finish reducing pressure.
5. Arrange ribs on a heatproof platter.
6. Thicken sauce, if necessary, by
boiling rapidly, uncovered, for a few
minutes. Pour over spareribs. If desired,
heat spareribs in a hot (450° F) oven for
5 minutes or run under the broiler for 2
minutes until they turn a dark brown.

**Serves 2 or 3 as a main dish; serves 6
as an appetizer (2½- to 8-quart
cooker).**

Lancashire Hot Pot

6 shoulder lamb chops, ½ inch thick
1 tablespoon oil
1 cup chicken or beef stock or
    bouillon or water
6 potatoes, peeled and sliced
3 onions, sliced
1 teaspoon salt
¼ teaspoon pepper
2 tablespoons butter or margarine

1. Trim fat from chops. Heat oil in cooker
and brown chops on both sides. Remove.
2. Pour stock into cooker. Alternate
layers of chops, potatoes and onions on
rack in cooker, sprinkling each layer with
salt and pepper. Dot top with butter.

3. Cover, set control at 10 and place over
high heat until control jiggles. Reduce
heat and cook 14 minutes (or cook at 15
for 10 minutes).
4. Remove from heat and let cool 5
minutes; then run cold water over the
cooker to finish reducing pressure.

Serves 4 to 6 (2½- or 4-quart cooker).
This recipe can be doubled in a 6- or
8-quart cooker; overlap chops if
necessary.

Lamb Curry

¼ cup oil
2½ pounds boneless lamb, cut
    into 1-inch cubes
2 to 3 tablespoons curry powder
1 teaspoon salt
½ teaspoon ginger
¼ teaspoon pepper
1 cup chopped onion
2 large apples, peeled and diced
1½ cups chicken stock or bouillon
2 tablespoons tomato paste
2 tablespoons heavy cream

1. Heat oil in cooker; brown lamb. Add
curry powder, salt, ginger and pepper;
cook, stirring, until the smell of curry is
very strong but not burned.
2. Add onion, apples, stock and tomato
paste.
3. Cover, set control at 10 and place over
high heat until control jiggles. Reduce
heat and cook 15 minutes (or cook at 15
for 12 minutes).
4. Remove from heat and let cool 5
minutes; then run cold water over the
cooker to finish reducing pressure.
5. Stir in heavy cream.
6. Serve with rice and traditional curry
accompaniments—bowls of chutney,
coconut, raisins, peanuts, diced
cucumber.

Serves 6 to 8 (4- to 8-quart cooker).
For a 2½-quart cooker, cut the recipe in
half. This recipe can also be doubled in
a 6- or 8-quart cooker.

tip

Unless you are an "old
hand" at using a pressure
cooker, it's a good idea to
use a bit more liquid than
the recipe specifies,
especially in the preparation
of meats. (After meats are
browned in hot oil, there is a
possibility that some of the
liquid you add may go up in
steam before the cover is
closed.)

Some of these recipes have
purposely recommended a
generous amount of liquid
to compensate for the
inexperience of those new
to using a pressure cooker.
As you learn to adjust the
heat properly (the control
should jiggle no more than 3
to 4 times a minute), you
may find you can reduce the
amount of liquid called for.

menu idea

*Oxtail Ragout Seville
(this page)*

Gnocchi (page 31)

Pears and Cheese

Oxtail Ragout Seville

2 tablespoons oil
2 oxtails (about 1½ pounds), cut into
   1-inch pieces
2 teaspoons chili powder
2 teaspoons prepared mustard
1 teaspoon cornstarch
¼ teaspoon salt
½ cup seedless raisins
1 cup water
1 cup orange juice
3 tablespoons lemon juice
1 tablespoon Worcestershire sauce
¼ cup pitted green olives, halved

1. Heat oil in cooker; brown oxtails on all sides.
2. Mix chili powder, mustard, cornstarch and salt; blend with raisins, water, juices and Worcestershire. Add mixture to meat.
3. Cover, set control at 10 and place over high heat until control jiggles. Reduce heat and cook 45 minutes (or cook at 15 for 35 minutes).
4. Remove from heat and let cool 5 minutes; then run cold water over the cooker to finish reducing pressure.
5. Add olives and heat through.

Serves 2 or 3 (2½- to 8-quart cooker). This recipe can be doubled in a 6- or 8-quart cooker.

Chicken Javanese

4 tablespoons butter or margarine
1 roasting chicken (about
   4 pounds)
1 teaspoon curry powder (or more to
   taste)
2 tablespoons peanut butter
1 cup chicken stock or bouillon
¼ cup evaporated milk
1 teaspoon flour
¼ teaspoon salt
   Pinch of pepper
   Juice of ½ lemon

1. Heat butter in cooker and brown chicken on all sides. Remove.
2. Add curry powder and peanut butter to the cooker and cook, stirring constantly, 2 minutes.
3. Add stock, evaporated milk, flour, salt and pepper. Stir until blended.
4. Place chicken on rack in cooker.
5. Cover, set control at 10 and place over high heat until control jiggles. Reduce heat and cook 20 to 25 minutes (or cook at 15 for 16 to 20 minutes).
6. Remove from heat and let cool 5 minutes; then run cold water over the cooker to finish reducing pressure.
7. Transfer chicken to a serving platter. Remove rack. Stir lemon juice into sauce and adjust seasoning. Spoon over chicken.

Serves 4 (2½- to 8-quart cooker).

Coq au Vin

1 broiler-fryer chicken, cut into 8
   pieces
1 teaspoon salt
  Pinch of pepper
2 tablespoons oil
8 small whole white onions, peeled
1 clove garlic, minced
1 can (4 ounces) sliced mushrooms,
   with liquid
1 cup red wine
¼ cup minced parsley
3 green onions, sliced
1 large bay leaf

1. Season chicken pieces with salt and pepper. Heat oil in cooker; brown chicken and remove. Add onions and garlic; cook, stirring, until onions are translucent.
2. Add chicken and remaining ingredients.
3. Cover, set control at 10 and place over high heat until control jiggles. Reduce heat and cook 15 minutes (or cook at 15 for 12 minutes).
4. Remove from heat and let cool 5 minutes; then run cold water over the cooker to finish reducing pressure.

Serves 4 (2½- or 4-quart cooker).
For a 6- or 8-quart cooker, use 1½ cups red wine.

Paella Valenciana

¼ cup olive oil
1 broiler-fryer chicken, cut into 8 or
   more serving pieces
1 onion, chopped
1 green pepper, seeded and
   chopped
1 clove garlic, chopped
1½ cups regular rice
½ teaspoon saffron threads
1 tablespoon hot water
2 large tomatoes (or 2 cups canned)
1 teaspoon salt
½ teaspoon pepper
  Pinch of crushed red pepper
3 cups water
1 pound raw shrimp, peeled and
   deveined

1. Heat oil in cooker; brown chicken lightly. Remove chicken.
2. Add onion, green pepper and garlic to cooker; cook, stirring, until onion is translucent. Add rice, saffron soaked in hot water, the chicken and the remaining ingredients except shrimp.
3. Cover, set control at 10 and place over high heat until control jiggles. Reduce heat and cook 15 minutes (or cook at 15 for 12 minutes).
4. Remove from heat and let cool 5 minutes; then run cold water over the cooker to finish reducing pressure.
5. Add shrimp. Cook, uncovered, a minute or two, depending on their size, just until shrimp are opaque.

Serves 6 (2½- to 8-quart cooker).

Kasha Varnishkas

1 cup kasha (roasted buckwheat kernels)
1 egg, beaten
2 cups water
1 teaspoon salt
3 tablespoons butter or margarine
1 onion, minced
1 cup noodle shells, cooked

1. Place kasha in skillet and cook, stirring, over *moderate* heat until warm. Add egg and continue to stir until grains are dry and separate.
2. Pour water into cooker and bring to a boil. Add kasha and salt.
3. Cover, set control at 15 and place over high heat until control jiggles. Reduce heat and cook 1 minute.
4. Run cold water over the cooker to reduce pressure instantly.
5. Melt butter in skillet and cook onion until golden. Add onion and noodles to kasha and heat through.

Serves 4 to 6 (2½- to 8-quart cooker).

Chinese Steamed Fish

1 sea bass or bluefish (2 pounds)
1 teaspoon finely grated gingerroot or ¼ teaspoon ground ginger
2 tablespoons sherry
2 tablespoons soy sauce
1½ tablespoons oil

1. Clean and scale fish; leave head and tail intact, Chinese style, if you like.
2. Place fish on a heatproof plate that will fit on rack in cooker. Sprinkle with ginger, sherry, soy and oil.
3. Pour 1½ cups hot water into cooker. Place plate on rack in cooker.
4. Cover, set control at 10 and place over high heat until control jiggles. Reduce heat and cook 5 minutes (or cook at 15 for 4 minutes).
5. Run cold water over the cooker to reduce pressure instantly.
6. Serve fish on cooking plate.

Serves 4 (2½- to 8-quart cooker).

Swedish Fish Pudding

¾ pound fillet of cod or other white-fleshed fish
2 eggs, lightly beaten
¼ cup heavy cream
¼ cup butter or margarine
⅓ cup flour
1 cup milk
1½ teaspoons salt
1 tablespoon lemon juice
Mustard Sauce (below)

1. Put the fish through the finest blade of the meat grinder. Add eggs and cream; blend well. (Or blend fish, cut up, in a blender, with eggs and cream.)
2. Melt butter in a saucepan; stir in flour. Gradually add milk and cook, stirring, until sauce is thickened and smooth.
3. Add sauce to fish mixture, a spoonful at a time, blending well after each addition. Season with salt and lemon juice.
4. Turn fish mixture into a buttered 4-cup metal mold. Cover with foil.
5. Pour 2 cups hot water into cooker. Place mold on rack in cooker.
6. Cover, set control at 5 and place over high heat until control jiggles. Reduce heat and cook 30 minutes (or cook at 15 for 18 minutes).
7. Run cold water over the cooker to reduce pressure instantly.
8. Unmold fish pudding on a platter. Serve hot or cold, with Mustard Sauce.

Serves 4 (2½- to 8-quart cooker).

Mustard Sauce

3 tablespoons mayonnaise
1 tablespoon prepared mustard
1 tablespoon drained capers

Combine all ingredients and mix thoroughly.

MONEY-SAVING MAIN DISHES

It's easy to be thrifty when you have all the time in the world to shop for specials and simmer for hours. But today's cooks live in a constant time squeeze. So, while it has always been known that such reliable fare as Stuffed Cabbage, Potted Beef Brisket and Chicken and Dumplings are as delicious as they are cost-conscious, most busy cooks couldn't afford the time required to make them.

Now, thanks to the pressure cooker, you can make short work of these budget beaters — and a dozen others, like Lemon Lamb Shanks, Sweet-Sour Tongue and Lentil Casserole. Less-tender, less-expensive cuts of meat become tender in no time. Even frozen turkey parts, a once-upon-a-time problem for after-work cooks, can be a part of your everyday menus.

menu idea

Dilly Beans (p. 123)
or
Green Beans Vinaigrette

Potted Beef Brisket (this page)

Potato Pancakes   Applesauce

Gingerbread
or
Compote of Dried Fruits
(p. 105)

Potted Beef Brisket

2½ pounds brisket of beef, trimmed
    of fat
2 cups red wine
1 teaspoon mixed pickling spice,
    tied in cheesecloth
2 tablespoons shortening
1 teaspoon salt
¼ teaspoon pepper
3 onions, sliced
½ cup sliced celery
2 carrots, sliced
½ cup water

1. Place brisket in a shallow bowl with wine and spice bag. Let stand at room temperature about 2 hours, turning often to season evenly, or refrigerate, covered, overnight.
2. Heat shortening in cooker; brown meat on all sides. Season with salt and pepper. Remove.
3. Add marinade and remaining ingredients to cooker, stirring in the brown bits that cling to the side.
4. Place meat on rack in cooker.
5. Cover, set control at 10 and place over high heat until control jiggles. Reduce heat and cook 1 hour (or cook at 15 for 50 minutes).
6. Remove from heat and let cool 5 minutes; then run cold water over the cooker to finish reducing pressure.
7. Transfer meat to a carving board. Carve across the grain into thin strips.
8. Discard spice bag and force gravy and vegetables through a sieve (or whirl in an electric blender).
9. Heat sauce and adjust seasoning to taste. Reheat meat slices in sauce.

Serves 6 (2½- to 8-quart cooker).

Stuffed Cabbage

1 large head Savoy cabbage
1½ pounds ground beef
1 onion, chopped
1 cup cooked rice
3 cans (8 ounces each) tomato
    sauce
1 teaspoon caraway seed
2 teaspoons salt
½ teaspoon pepper
2 cups water
3 tablespoons lemon juice
½ cup raisins
3 tablespoons brown sugar

1. Wash cabbage and discard tough outer leaves. Cut a slice from the top of the cabbage and scoop out the inside, leaving a thick shell.
2. Shred enough of the scooped-out cabbage to measure 1 cup. Reserve remaining cabbage for other uses.
3. Brown meat in a skillet, stirring with a fork. Drain off excess fat. Add onion and shredded cabbage and cook, stirring, until vegetables are wilted. Add rice, 1 can of tomato sauce, caraway seed, salt and pepper.
4. Fill the cabbage hollow with meat mixture. Wrap cabbage in a foil pouch, leaving the top open.
5. In cooker, mix remaining 2 cans of tomato sauce with water, lemon juice and raisins. Place cabbage on rack in cooker.
6. Cover, set control at 15 and place over high heat until control jiggles. Reduce heat and cook 10 minutes.
7. Run cold water over the cooker to reduce pressure instantly.
8. Transfer cabbage to a serving platter and remove foil.
9. Boil sauce rapidly, uncovered, to thicken to desired consistency. Add brown sugar and adjust seasoning to taste. Pour sauce over cabbage, cut into wedges.

Serves 6 to 8 (6- or 8-quart cooker).

Meat Loaf

1½ pounds ground beef chuck
2 eggs, slightly beaten
1 cup soft rye bread crumbs
½ cup minced onion
2 tablespoons chopped parsley
1 tablespoon horseradish
2 teaspoons salt
½ teaspoon dry mustard
2 tablespoons milk
1 can (8 ounces) tomato sauce
2 tablespoons Worcestershire sauce
1½ pounds scrubbed new potatoes
   (optional)

1. Stir meat and eggs together with a fork. Add bread crumbs, onion, parsley, horseradish, salt, dry mustard, milk and half the tomato sauce. Combine lightly but thoroughly.
2. Stir Worcestershire sauce with remaining tomato sauce and spread 4 tablespoons in the bottom of an 8½ x 4½ x 2½-inch loaf pan.
3. Turn meat mixture into loaf pan. Spread remaining sauce over meat.
4. Pour 2 cups water into cooker. Place loaf pan on rack in cooker.
5. Peel a strip from around the middle of each potato and place on rack around meat loaf.
6. Cover, set control at 10 and place over high heat until control jiggles. Reduce heat and cook 18 minutes (or cook at 15 for 15 minutes).
7. Remove from heat and let cool 5 minutes; then run cold water over the cooker to finish reducing pressure.

Serves 6 (6- or 8-quart cooker).
For a 2½- or 4-quart cooker, use a 6-cup mold to fit cooker; use 1 cup water in Step 4.

Meatball Stew

1 pound ground beef or meat loaf
   mixture
½ cup soft bread crumbs
1 egg
¼ cup chopped onion
½ teaspoon mixed herbs
1 teaspoon salt
½ teaspoon pepper
2 tablespoons oil
12 small carrots, scraped
4 medium potatoes, peeled
2 large onions, quartered
¾ cup water
1 beef bouillon cube

1. Mix meat with bread crumbs, egg, onion, herbs, salt and pepper. Shape into 12 balls.
2. Heat oil in cooker; brown meatballs on all sides.
3. Arrange vegetables on top of meatballs. Add water and bouillon cube.
4. Cover, set control at 10 and place over high heat until control jiggles. Reduce heat and cook 15 minutes (or cook at 15 for 12 minutes).
5. Run cold water over the cooker to reduce pressure instantly.
6. If gravy seems too thin, transfer meat and vegetables to a serving bowl with a slotted spoon. Boil gravy rapidly, uncovered, to thicken it; pour over the meat and vegetables.

Serves 4 (2½- to 8-quart cooker).
This recipe can be doubled in a 6- or 8-quart cooker.

Spaghetti
and Meatballs

1 pound lean ground beef
1 pound pork sausage meat
1 clove garlic, minced
¼ cup chopped parsley
2 tablespoons milk
2 eggs, beaten
1 teaspoon salt
1 teaspoon pepper
4 tablespoons bacon fat or oil
2 cloves garlic, chopped
1 onion, chopped
½ green pepper, seeded and chopped
1 can (6 ounces) tomato paste
1 can (16 ounces) tomatoes, with
   liquid
½ teaspoon oregano
2 whole cloves
1 bay leaf
1 can (4 ounces) sliced mushrooms,
   with liquid
1 cup water
1 pound spaghetti, cooked

1. Blend beef, sausage, garlic, parsley, milk, eggs, salt and pepper. Shape into 2- to 2½-inch balls.
2. Heat 2 tablespoons of the bacon fat in cooker; brown meatballs on all sides. Remove and reserve.
3. Add remaining 2 tablespoons fat to cooker. Cook garlic, onion and green pepper until onion is golden.
4. Add remaining ingredients except spaghetti and meatballs and bring to a boil.
5. Add browned meatballs.
6. Cover, set control at 10 and place over high heat until control jiggles. Reduce heat and cook 12 minutes (or cook at 15 for 8 minutes).
7. Remove from heat and let cool 5 minutes. Run cold water over the cooker to finish reducing pressure. Serve over hot cooked spaghetti.

Serves 6 (6- or 8-quart cooker).
For a 2½- or 4-quart cooker, cut the recipe in half.

Meat Sauce
for Spaghetti

3 slices bacon
¾ cup chopped onion
2 cloves garlic, chopped
1 pound lean ground beef
1 can (20 ounces) solid-pack
   tomatoes
1 can (6 ounces) tomato paste
1½ cups water
1 teaspoon basil
1 teaspoon oregano
1 bay leaf
1 teaspoon salt
1 teaspoon sugar
   Pinch of cayenne pepper

1. Brown bacon in cooker; remove and crumble.
2. Cook onion and garlic in bacon fat until onion is translucent.
3. Add beef and cook, stirring, until beef loses its red color.
4. Add tomatoes, tomato paste, water, basil, oregano and bay leaf.
5. Cover, set control at 10 and place over high heat until control jiggles. Reduce heat and cook 36 minutes (or cook at 15 for 30 minutes).
6. Run cold water over the cooker to reduce pressure instantly.
7. Thicken sauce, if necessary, by cooking over high heat, stirring. Season with salt, sugar and cayenne. (This is enough sauce for about 1 pound of spaghetti.)

About 1 quart (4- to 8-quart cooker).
For a 2½-quart cooker, cut the recipe in half. This recipe can also be doubled in a 6- or 8-quart cooker.

tip

To make the most out of your meat dollars, forget all about the price per pound — instead, buy by the price per serving. Here's how to figure: For meats with a bone, 2 or 3 servings per pound (only 1 or 2 servings, if large-boned); for boneless meats, 4 servings per pound.

Sweet-Sour Tongue

1 smoked tongue (about 4 pounds)
2 tablespoons mixed pickling spice
Sweet-Sour Sauce (below)

1. Place tongue in cooker and cover with cold water; bring to a boil, without covering. Remove from heat. Drain off the water and taste; if it is very salty, repeat refreshing process. Drain again.
2. Pour 2 cups water into cooker and add spice. Place tongue in cooker.
3. Cover, set control at 10 and place over high heat until control jiggles. Reduce heat and cook 1 hour (or cook at 15 for 45 minutes).
4. Remove from heat and let pressure reduce naturally.
5. Peel off tongue skin and trim away fat and gristle. Slice thinly. Strain tongue broth and reserve 3 cups to make sauce.

Serves 6 to 8 (4- to 8-quart cooker).

Sweet-Sour Sauce

1½ tablespoons cornstarch
¼ cup cold water
3 cups strained tongue broth
⅓ cup raisins
⅓ cup brown sugar
1½ tablespoons molasses
¼ cup lemon juice

1. Mix cornstarch with the cold water to make a paste. Combine the paste and tongue broth in a saucepan; heat and stir until sauce is thickened.
2. Add remaining ingredients. Simmer 5 minutes, stirring often.
3. Season to taste with salt, pepper, more sugar and lemon juice.
4. Spoon sauce over slices of hot tongue, or reheat sliced tongue in sauce.

Tripe, Southern Style

2½ pounds tripe
1 cup water
2 tablespoons salt
2 tablespoons oil
1 clove garlic, minced
1 onion, sliced
1 green pepper, seeded and sliced
½ teaspoon oregano
¼ teaspoon thyme
1 can (16 ounces) tomatoes, drained and chopped

1. Cut tripe into 1-inch strips. Put into cooker with water and salt.
2. Cover, set control at 10 and place over high heat until control jiggles. Reduce heat and cook 15 minutes (or cook at 15 for 12 minutes).
3. Remove from heat and let cool 5 minutes; then run cold water over the cooker to finish reducing pressure.
4. Drain tripe, reserving cooking liquid.
5. To make sauce, heat oil in cooker; add garlic, onion and green pepper and cook until onion is translucent.
6. Add ½ cup tripe liquid, the oregano, thyme and tomatoes. Simmer 5 minutes over low heat. Thicken sauce, if necessary, by cooking rapidly, uncovered. Adjust seasoning to taste.
7. Heat tripe in sauce. Serve over hot cooked noodles or rice.

Serves 4 (2½- to 8-quart cooker).

Tripe Lyonnaise

2½ pounds tripe
2 onions, sliced
½ cup butter or margarine
2 tablespoons chopped parsley
1½ tablespoons white wine vinegar

1. Follow steps 1 through 3 of Tripe, Southern Style. Drain and dry cooked tripe strips.
2. Cook onions in butter until translucent. Add remaining ingredients and stir until heated through. Pour over tripe.

Lemon Lamb Shanks

3 tablespoons oil
4 lamb shanks
    (about ½ pound each)
½ cup white wine
1 cup chicken stock, bouillon or
    water
1 tablespoon grated lemon peel
1 teaspoon salt
½ teaspoon pepper
½ teaspoon sugar
1 clove garlic, crushed
½ cup chopped parsley
    Thin lemon slices

1. Heat oil in cooker and brown lamb shanks. Add wine, stock and lemon peel; sprinkle with salt, pepper and sugar.
2. Cover, set control at 10 and place over high heat until control jiggles. Reduce heat and cook 25 minutes (or cook at 15 for 20 minutes).
3. Remove from heat and let cool 5 minutes; then run cold water over the cooker to finish reducing pressure.
4. Remove lamb to serving platter. Add garlic to cooker; boil sauce rapidly, uncovered, to thicken.
5. Add parsley and spoon over shanks. Garnish with lemon slices. Serve with rice.

Serves 4 (6- or 8-quart cooker).
For a 2½- or 4-quart cooker, cut the recipe in half.

NOTE:
If using larger lamb shanks (about 12 ounces each), set control at 10 and cook 35 minutes (or cook at 15 for 30 minutes).

Lamb and Lima Beans

2 cups small dried lima beans
2 tablespoons oil
1½ pounds lamb, cut into 1-inch cubes
¾ cup chopped onion
1 clove garlic, minced
1 can (28 ounces) solid-pack
    tomatoes
¾ cup water
1 teaspoon salt
¼ teaspoon pepper
¼ cup chopped parsley

1. Par-cook, soak and drain beans (page 26); reserve.
2. Heat oil in cooker; brown lamb cubes on all sides.
3. Add onion and garlic and cook, stirring, until onion is translucent. Add tomatoes and water.
4. Cover, set control at 10 and place over high heat until control jiggles. Reduce heat and cook 15 to 20 minutes (or cook at 15 for 12 to 15 minutes).
5. Run cold water over the cooker to reduce pressure instantly.
6. Open cooker and add lima beans.
7. Cover, set control at 15 and place over high heat until control jiggles. Reduce heat and cook 2 minutes.
8. Remove from heat and let cool 5 minutes; then run cold water over the cooker to finish reducing pressure.
9. Thicken sauce, if necessary, by boiling rapidly, uncovered. Add salt and pepper. Serve sprinkled with chopped parsley.

Serves 4 (2½- to 8-quart cooker).

Chicken and Dumplings

2 tablespoons butter or margarine
1 broiler-fryer chicken, cut into
    serving pieces
1 onion, chopped
1½ cups water
1 carrot, scraped
¼ teaspoon salt
    Pinch of pepper
1 tablespoon mixed pickling spice,
    tied in cheesecloth
    Dumplings (below)

1. Heat butter in cooker; brown chicken and onion lightly, turning often.
2. Add water, carrot, salt, pepper and pickling spice.
3. Cover, set control at 10 and place over high heat until control jiggles. Reduce heat and cook 15 minutes (or cook at 15 for 12 minutes).
4. Remove from heat and let cool 5 minutes; then run cold water over the cooker to finish reducing pressure.
5. Top chicken with dumpling batter and cook, uncovered, 5 minutes.
6. Cover, place over heat and allow a small stream of steam to escape from vent tube for 5 minutes.
7. Run cold water over the cooker until steam no longer escapes from vent tube.

Serves 4 (4- to 8-quart cooker).
For a 2½-quart cooker, omit Dumplings.

Dumplings

2 cups flour
2 teaspoons baking powder
1 teaspoon salt
1 tablespoon butter or margarine
1 cup milk

1. Mix flour, baking powder and salt.
2. Cut in butter. Add milk and mix until flour is thoroughly dampened. Mixture will not be smooth.
3. Drop spoonfuls of batter onto chicken in cooker. Cook as directed above.

Poached Turkey Breast

½ turkey breast (about 3 pounds)
2 cups water
1 teaspoon salt
3 large onions, cut into wedges
2 stalks celery, with leafy tops
3 sprigs of parsley
2 carrots, scraped
    Sauce (below)

1. Place turkey breast half in cooker, meaty side down. Add water and remaining ingredients except sauce.
2. Cover, set control at 10 and place over high heat until control jiggles. Reduce heat and cook 25 minutes (or cook at 15 for 20 minutes).
3. Remove from heat and let cool 5 minutes; then run cold water over the cooker to finish reducing pressure.
4. Remove turkey to platter; slice. Reserve broth to make sauce.

Serves 4 to 6 (4- to 8-quart cooker).
A 3-pound turkey breast half can be cooked in a 2½-quart cooker providing there is at least a 1-inch space between the meat and the top of the cooker.

Sauce

Turkey broth (above)
2 tablespoons sherry
2 teaspoons soy sauce
2 tablespoons cornstarch

1. Strain broth and return to cooker. Reserve carrots and slice.
2. Mix sherry, soy and cornstarch to make a paste. Add to broth and cook, stirring, until thickened and clear. Add carrots and heat. Pour sauce over turkey on platter.

Poached Turkey Legs

Cook 3 uniform turkey legs, about 1 pound each, as directed for Poached Turkey Breast, but reduce cooking time to 12 minutes at 10 pounds pressure or 10 minutes at 15 pounds pressure.

menu idea

Cranberry Juice Cocktail

*Poached Turkey Breast
(this page)*

*Sweet Potato Casserole (p. 80)
or Mashed Sweet Potatoes*

Brownies with Ice Cream

Codfish Cakes

1 pound salt codfish
1½ pounds medium potatoes
¼ small onion, grated
¼ teaspoon white pepper
1 egg
¼ lemon, with peel
　Oil for deep-fat frying

1. Cover fish with boiling water; let stand 20 minutes.
2. Meanwhile, pour 1½ cups water into cooker. Scrub potatoes but do not peel; place on rack in cooker.
3. Cover, set control at 15 and place over high heat until control jiggles. Reduce heat and cook 15 minutes.
4. Run cold water over the cooker to reduce pressure instantly.
5. Drain potatoes; peel and mash. Season with onion and white pepper. Beat in egg. Reserve.
6. Drain codfish and place on rack in cooker. Add boiling water to cover. Add lemon wedge.
7. Cover, set control at 15 and place over high heat until control jiggles. Reduce heat and cook 7 minutes.
8. Run cold water over the cooker to reduce pressure instantly.
9. Drain fish and shred; blend with mashed potatoes. Adjust seasoning to taste.
10. Heat oil (1 inch deep) in a skillet. Drop codfish mixture by spoonfuls into hot oil (375° F); fry until crisply browned.

Serves 6 (2½- to 8-quart cooker).

Codfish Potato Puff

1. Follow Steps 1 through 9 of Codfish Cakes except use 2 eggs, separated, in Step 5. Beat in yolks; beat whites until stiff and then fold in.
2. Turn mixture into a buttered 6-cup metal mold. Cover with foil.
3. Pour 2 cups water into cooker. Place mold on rack in cooker.
4. Cover, set control at 15 and place over high heat until control jiggles. Reduce heat and cook 12 minutes.
5. Run cold water over the cooker to reduce pressure instantly.
6. If desired, sprinkle top of puff with buttered bread crumbs and brown quickly under the broiler.

Serves 6 (6- or 8-quart cooker).
A 2½- or 4-quart cooker can be used if your mold fits.

Lentil Casserole

2 cups dried lentils
4 slices bacon, diced
1 small onion, minced
1 quart water
1 tablespoon chopped parsley
1 tablespoon salt
¼ teaspoon pepper
1 tablespoon wine vinegar

1. Wash and drain lentils; reserve.
2. Cook bacon in cooker only until some of the fat has been rendered. Do not allow bacon to become browned or crisp.
3. Add onion; cook until translucent.
4. Add lentils, water, parsley, salt, pepper and wine vinegar.
5. Cover, set control at 15 and place over high heat until control jiggles. Reduce heat and cook 15 minutes.
6. Remove from heat and let cool 5 minutes; then run cold water over the cooker to finish reducing pressure.
7. Adjust seasoning to taste.

Serves 6 (2½- to 8-quart cooker).

A change-of-pace dinner idea; easy on the budget, too — Lemon Lamb Shanks (page 50).

Chinese Beef and Peppers (page 38) — dinner-party fare with an Oriental flair.

For hearty, flavorful stick-to-the-ribs goodness — Meatball Stew (page 47).

High on style but low on calories — Steamed Bass with Vegetables (page 64).

ESPECIALLY FOR CALORIE COUNTERS

Beef Stroganoff, Curried Lamb Chops, Buttermilk Chicken, Fisherman's Stew, even Marmalade Soufflé — can these be meant for a calorie counter? Indeed. And with recipes like these, you'll find that calorie counting can become a comfortable way of cooking, a delicious way of eating.

The recipes on the following pages have been specifically designed to meet the low-calorie needs of the dieter and the high-in-flavor needs of the non-dieter. So there's no need to cook a "special" meal for the one who's watching his weight. Nor is there any need to stick to a boring regime. Learn to rely on foods that are low in calories — use more chicken and fish, avoid rich sauces, satisfy your sweet tooth with fruits. It's really a matter of common sense.

While you are modifying your cooking habits in regard to ingredients, you'll also find that changing to the pressure cooking technique makes it easy to avoid the temptation of tasting as you cook. Pressure cooker dishes jiggle away, closed, until it's mealtime — so soon after the beginning, there's hardly time to steal a snack!

Beef-Stuffed Zucchini

2 medium zucchini (about ½ pound
   each)
½ pound ground beef
2 tablespoons finely chopped onion
1 clove garlic, minced
2 tablespoons pine nuts
½ teaspoon marjoram
½ teaspoon salt
¼ teaspoon pepper
1 egg, slightly beaten

1. Scrub zucchini and remove ends. Cut
in half lengthwise. Scoop out pulp,
leaving a shell ¼ inch thick. Reserve
shells and chop pulp.
2. Cook meat in a skillet, stirring
constantly, until it loses its red color.
Add chopped zucchini, onion and garlic;
cook, stirring, until onion is golden. Add
remaining ingredients and blend well.
3. Fill zucchini shells with mixture. Wrap
shells in foil, leaving the top open.
4. Pour 1 cup water into cooker. Place
stuffed zucchini packet on rack in
cooker.
5. Cover, set control at 10 and place
over high heat until control jiggles.
Reduce heat and cook 8 minutes (or
cook at 15 for 6 minutes).
6. Run cold water over the cooker to
reduce pressure instantly.

Calories: 185 per serving.
Serves 4 (4- to 8-quart cooker).
Depending on shape of the zucchini,
recipe may be used in 2½-quart cooker.

Beef Stroganoff

1 pound thin-sliced round steak or
   sirloin tip
2 tablespoons oil
½ cup chopped onion
1 teaspoon salt
¼ teaspoon pepper
   Pinch of nutmeg
1 can (4 ounces) mushrooms, with
   liquid
1 cup beef bouillon
½ cup tomato juice
2 tablespoons flour
½ cup plain yogurt

1. Cut beef into thin strips.
2. Heat oil in cooker and brown beef.
Add onion, salt, pepper and nutmeg.
Cook, stirring, until onion is translucent.
3. Add mushrooms, bouillon and tomato
juice.
4. Cover, set control at 10 and place
over high heat until control jiggles.
Reduce heat and cook 10 minutes (or
cook at 15 for 8 minutes).
5. Remove from heat and let cool 5
minutes; then run cold water over the
cooker to finish reducing pressure.
6. Blend flour with a little water (about ¼
cup); add to cooker and cook, stirring,
until sauce is smooth. Remove from
heat and blend in yogurt.

Calories: 250 per serving.
Serves 4 (2½- to 8-quart cooker).

Veal Birds

1 pound boneless veal, sliced thin
    (about 4 slices)
1 teaspoon salt
    Pinch of pepper
1 whole dill pickle, minced
1 onion, minced
½ teaspoon garlic powder
½ cup bread crumbs
1 tablespoon butter or margarine
1 cup tomato juice
½ cup water

1. Pound veal slices between sheets of waxed paper to flatten. Sprinkle with salt and pepper.
2. Mix pickle, onion, garlic powder and crumbs. Spread filling over flattened veal slices. Roll up and secure with wooden picks.
3. Melt butter in cooker; brown veal rolls. Add tomato juice and water.
4. Cover, set control at 10 and place over high heat until control jiggles. Reduce heat and cook 10 minutes (or cook at 15 for 8 minutes).
5. Remove from heat and let cool 5 minutes; then run cold water over the cooker to finish reducing pressure.

Calories: 275 per serving.
Serves 4 (2½- to 8-quart cooker).

Curried Lamb Chops

4 shoulder lamb chops (4 ounces each)
2 medium onions, diced
2 small apples, diced
2 teaspoons curry powder
1 cup chicken bouillon
¼ teaspoon cinnamon
¼ teaspoon pepper

1. Trim fat from chops. Heat cooker and rub bottom with trimmed fat just until coated (or use a nonstick spray). Brown chops and remove from cooker; discard all but 1 tablespoon of the drippings.
2. Add onions and apples. Sprinkle with curry powder and cook, stirring, until onions are soft. Do not burn the curry.
3. Add bouillon, cinnamon and pepper. Stir, scraping in all the brown bits.
4. Return chops to the cooker; spoon sauce over chops.
5. Cover, set control at 10 and place over high heat until control jiggles. Reduce heat and cook 7 minutes (or cook at 15 for 5 minutes).
6. Remove from heat and let cool 5 minutes; then run cold water over the cooker to finish reducing pressure.

Calories: 235 per serving.
Serves 4 (2½- or 4-quart cooker).
For a 6- or 8-quart cooker, use 1½ cups chicken bouillon.

Buttermilk Chicken

1 broiler-fryer chicken, cut into 8 pieces
2 tablespoons chopped onion
1 teaspoon salt
1 teaspoon paprika
½ teaspoon garlic powder
½ teaspoon pepper
¼ teaspoon cumin
½ cup buttermilk
1 cup tomato sauce
1 tablespoon prepared mustard

1. Remove skin from chicken pieces and discard.
2. Sprinkle chicken with onion and seasonings. Cover and refrigerate 1 to 1½ hours.
3. Place chicken in cooker. Combine buttermilk, tomato sauce and mustard; pour over chicken.
4. Cover, set control at 10 and place over high heat until control jiggles. Reduce heat and cook 15 minutes (or cook at 15 for 12 minutes).
5. Remove from heat and let cool 5 minutes; then run cold water over the cooker to finish reducing pressure.

Calories: 260 per serving.
Serves 4 (2½- to 8-quart cooker).

tip

Leaving the skin on the chicken adds 70 calories for every 3 ounces of meat. And that can really add up.

menu idea

Tossed Green Salad

Savory Chicken (this page)

Low-Calorie Orange Sherbet

Savory Chicken

1 broiler-fryer chicken, cut into 8 pieces
½ cup lemon juice
¼ cup soy sauce
1 teaspoon pepper
1 tablespoon oil
2 medium onions, cut into wedges
4 medium potatoes, cut into wedges
4 medium green peppers, cut into wedges
1 cup tomato juice
½ cup water
1 bay leaf

1. Remove skin from chicken pieces and discard.
2. Combine lemon juice, soy sauce and pepper. Place chicken in soy mixture and turn to coat. Cover and refrigerate 2½ to 3 hours. Drain.
3. Heat oil in cooker; brown chicken. Add onions and brown lightly. Add remaining ingredients.
4. Cover, set control at 10 and place over high heat until control jiggles. Reduce heat and cook 12 minutes (or cook at 15 for 10 minutes.)
5. Remove from heat and let cool 5 minutes; then run cold water over the cooker to finish reducing pressure.
6. Discard bay leaf. Remove chicken and vegetables to a serving platter. Boil sauce rapidly to thicken, if necessary. Season to taste with salt and pepper. Pour sauce over chicken and vegetables.

Calories: 325 per serving.
Serves 4 (2½- to 8-quart cooker).

Lemon-Baked Chicken

2 whole chicken breasts (12 ounces each)
3 tablespoons lemon juice
¼ cup prepared mustard
1 tablespoon chopped parsley
1 teaspoon tarragon
½ teaspoon garlic powder
½ teaspoon salt
   Pinch of pepper
1 lemon, thinly sliced
   Paprika

1. Skin and bone chicken breasts; cut in half.
2. Mix 2 tablespoons of the lemon juice, the mustard, parsley, tarragon, garlic powder, salt and pepper; coat chicken with this mixture.
3. Arrange chicken in 1½-quart heatproof bowl. Top with lemon slices and sprinkle with remaining lemon juice and paprika.
4. Pour 1½ cups water into cooker. Place bowl on rack in cooker.
5. Cover, set control at 10 and place over high heat until control jiggles. Reduce heat and cook 15 minutes (or cook at 15 for 12 minutes).
6. Remove from heat and let cool 5 minutes; then run cold water over the cooker to finish reducing pressure.

Calories: 175 per serving.
Serves 4 (6- or 8-quart cooker).
A 2½- or 4-quart cooker can be used if your bowl fits; use 1 cup water in Step 4.

Chicken-Stuffed Cabbage Rolls

1 small green cabbage
1 cup diced cooked chicken
1 cup rolled oats
½ cup finely chopped celery
3 tablespoons finely chopped onion
2 tablespoons finely chopped
   parsley
1 egg, slightly beaten
½ teaspoon tarragon
¼ teaspoon paprika
1 teaspoon salt
¼ teaspoon pepper
⅓ cup white wine
⅔ cup chicken bouillon
1 tablespoon butter or margarine,
   softened
1 tablespoon flour

1. Remove 8 large leaves from cabbage. (Reserve remaining cabbage for another use.) Blanch the leaves in boiling salted water until soft. Cool under cold running water and drain.
2. Combine the chicken, rolled oats, vegetables, egg and seasonings.
3. Spoon ⅓ cup of chicken mixture onto the bottom edge of each cabbage leaf. Turn sides in and roll up loosely, jelly-roll fashion.
4. Pour wine and bouillon into cooker. Arrange cabbage rolls, seam side down, on rack in cooker.
5. Cover, set control at 10 and place over high heat until control jiggles. Reduce heat and cook 5 minutes (or cook at 15 for 4 minutes).
6. Remove from heat and let cool 5 minutes; then run cold water over the cooker to finish reducing pressure.
7. Arrange cabbage rolls on a heated serving platter. Remove rack.
8. Blend butter and flour into a smooth paste and add to sauce in cooker. Boil rapidly to thicken sauce, stirring constantly. Pour sauce over cabbage rolls.

Calories: 222 per serving.
Serves 4 (2½- to 8-quart cooker).

Lobster Tails

4 frozen lobster tails (4 ounces
   each)

1. Rinse frozen tails in cold water.
2. Pour ½ cup water into cooker. Place lobster tails on rack in cooker.
3. Cover, set control at 10 and place over high heat until control jiggles. Reduce heat and cook 2 minutes (or cook at 15 for 1 minute).
4. Run cold water over the cooker to reduce pressure instantly. Serve with lemon wedges.

Calories: 100 per lobster tail.
Serves 2 to 4 (2½- to 8-quart cooker).
This recipe can be doubled in a 6- or 8-quart cooker; use 1 cup water in Step 2.

Hearty Fish Soup

1 pound fish fillets
3 cups fish stock or clam broth
1 cup sliced carrots
1½ cups chopped celery
½ cup minced onion
2 tablespoons lemon juice
¼ teaspoon thyme
½ bay leaf
½ teaspoon salt
¼ teaspoon pepper

1. Combine all ingredients in cooker.
2. Cover, set control at 10 and place over high heat until control jiggles. Reduce heat and cook 8 minutes (or cook at 15 for 6 minutes).
3. Remove from heat and let cool 5 minutes; then run cold water over the cooker to finish reducing pressure.

Calories: 122 per serving.
Serves 4 (2½- to 8-quart cooker).

Fisherman's Stew

1½ pounds sole, cod or whiting fillets,
    cut into 2-inch pieces
1½ teaspoons salt
½ teaspoon pepper
1 cup clam broth
¼ cup dry white wine
1¼ cups chopped onion
1 clove garlic, chopped
1 cup chopped celery
2 tablespoons chopped parsley
¼ teaspoon ground saffron
1 tablespoon lemon juice

1. Place fish in a nonstick or lightly greased 6-cup metal mold, at least 4 inches deep. Sprinkle with salt and pepper.
2. Combine remaining ingredients and let stand 5 minutes. Pour over fish.
3. Pour 1½ cups water into cooker. Place mold on rack in cooker.
4. Cover, set control at 10 and place over high heat until control jiggles. Reduce heat and cook 5 minutes (or cook at 15 for 4 minutes).
5. Run cold water over the cooker to reduce pressure instantly.

Calories: 165 per serving.
Serves 4 (6- or 8-quart cooker).
A 2½- or 4-quart cooker can be used if your mold fits; use 1 cup water in Step 3.

NOTE:
The use of a mold is not essential in this recipe. If you prefer, you can cook the stew directly in the cooker — omit Step 3.

Fish Italiano

2 whitings or other white-fleshed fish
    (1 pound each), cleaned
2 teaspoons oil (preferably olive)
1 onion, chopped
1 clove garlic, minced
1 can (16 ounces) Italian-style
    tomatoes
¼ cup white wine
1 tablespoon chopped parsley
1 bay leaf
½ teaspoon salt
¼ teaspoon pepper
Pinch of oregano

1. Remove heads and tails of fish and reserve for stock. Cut each fish into 2 serving pieces; arrange in a 1-quart baking dish. (Pieces may overlap slightly.)
2. Heat oil in small saucepan; cook onion and garlic until onion is translucent.
3. Add tomatoes and remaining ingredients; simmer 5 minutes. Discard bay leaf and pour sauce over fish.
4. Pour 1 cup water into cooker. Place baking dish on rack in cooker.
5. Cover, set control at 10 and place over high heat until control jiggles. Reduce heat and cook 5 minutes (or cook at 15 for 4 minutes).
6. Run cold water over the cooker to reduce pressure instantly.

Calories: 275 per serving.
Serves 4 (2½- or 4-quart cooker).
For a 6- or 8-quart cooker, use 1½ cups water in Step 4.

Pompano Royale

4 pompano fillets (6 ounces each)
1 teaspoon salt
½ teaspoon pepper
2 tablespoons sherry
1 clove garlic, minced
1 cup sliced green onions
8 lemon slices
1 cucumber, sliced

1. Season pompano with salt and pepper. (Red snapper or sole may be substituted for the pompano if desired.) Arrange fish in a baking dish that will fit into cooker. (Fillets may overlap slightly.)
2. Combine sherry with garlic and onions; sprinkle over fish.
3. Pour 1 cup water into cooker. Place baking dish on rack in cooker.
4. Cover, set control at 10 and place over high heat until control jiggles. Reduce heat and cook 5 minutes (or cook at 15 for 4 minutes).
5. Run cold water over the cooker to reduce pressure instantly.
6. Garnish fish with lemon and cucumber slices.

Calories: 136 per serving.
Serves 4 (2½- or 4-quart cooker).
For a 6- or 8-quart cooker, use 1½ cups water in Step 3.

Spinach-Stuffed Sole

½ cup chopped onion
¼ pound mushrooms, sliced
1 tablespoon oil
1 teaspoon salt
¼ teaspoon sage
  Pinch of pepper
  Pinch of nutmeg
2 cups spinach, torn into pieces
6 sole fillets (6 ounces each)
  Juice of 2 lemons
3 medium tomatoes, cut into wedges
¼ cup low-calorie Italian dressing
2 tablespoons chopped parsley
  Lemon wedges

1. In saucepan sauté onion and mushrooms in oil. Remove from heat and add salt, sage, pepper and nutmeg. Mix with spinach.
2. Sprinkle fillets with lemon juice and top with vegetable mixture. Roll up and secure with wooden picks. Arrange in a high-sided baking dish that will fit into cooker.
3. Arrange tomatoes on fish. Brush all with dressing.
4. Pour 1 cup water into cooker. Set baking dish on rack in cooker.
5. Cover, set control at 10 and place over high heat until control jiggles. Reduce heat and cook 5 minutes (or cook at 15 for 4 minutes).
6. Run cold water over the cooker to reduce pressure instantly.
7. Serve garnished with chopped parsley and lemon wedges.

Calories: 200 per serving.
Serves 6 (2½- or 4-quart cooker).
For a 6- or 8-quart cooker, use 1½ cups water in Step 4.

menu idea

Mushroom Salad

Spinach-Stuffed Sole
(this page)

Stewed Peaches (p. 66)
or Fresh Fruit

Steamed Bass with Vegetables

4- to 5-pound whole sea bass
¾ cup white wine
¼ cup water
1 teaspoon salt
¼ teaspoon white pepper
3 carrrots, cut into sticks
2 stalks celery, cut into sticks
3 onions, cut into sticks
1 clove garlic, minced
1 bay leaf
1 tablespoon butter or margarine, softened
1 tablespoon flour

1 Clean bass but leave head and tail intact.
2. Pour wine and water into cooker.
3. Place fish on rack in cooker. Season with salt and pepper. Arrange carrots, celery, onions, garlic and bay leaf on fish.
4. Cover, set control at 10 and place over high heat until control jiggles. Reduce heat and cook 5 minutes (or cook at 15 for 4 minutes).
5. Remove from heat and let cool 5 minutes; then run cold water over the cooker to finish reducing pressure.
6. Remove fish and vegetables to a hot platter; discard bay leaf.
7. Blend butter and flour to make a smooth paste; add bit by bit to liquid in cooker. Stir over low heat until sauce is thick; pour over fish.

Calories: 300 per serving.
Serves 6 (6- or 8-quart cooker).
For a 2½- or 4-quart cooker, use a 1- to 3-pound fish and half the amounts of vegetables; all other ingredients remain the same.

Almond-Stuffed Mushrooms

12 large fresh mushrooms
 4 tablespoons chopped almonds
 2 cloves garlic, chopped
 1 tablespoon chopped fresh basil or 1 teaspoon dried
½ cup chopped onion
½ teaspoon salt
¼ teaspoon pepper
 2 tablespoons grated Parmesan cheese

1. Wipe mushroom caps and stems clean. Remove and chop stems; reserve caps. Combine chopped stems with remaining ingredients except cheese.
2. Fill mushroom caps with mixture; sprinkle with cheese. Arrange caps on greased heatproof plate and cover with foil.
3. Pour 1 cup water into cooker. Place plate on rack in cooker.
4. Cover, set control at 15 and place over high heat until control jiggles. Remove from heat at once.
5. Run cold water over the cooker to reduce pressure instantly.

Calories: 134 per serving.
Serves 4 (2½- or 4-quart cooker).
For a 6- or 8-quart cooker, use 1½ cups water in Step 3.

Country Red Cabbage

1 medium Bermuda onion, chopped
1 slice bacon, chopped
1 pound red cabbage, chopped
2 tart apples, peeled and cubed
½ cup water
1 chicken bouillon cube
3 tablespoons cider vinegar
1 teaspoon Worcestershire sauce
1 teaspoon caraway seed

1. Cook onion and bacon in cooker, stirring, until onion is wilted. Add remaining ingredients.
2. Cover, set control at 15 and place over high heat until control jiggles. Reduce heat and cook 5 minutes.
3. Run cold water over the cooker to reduce pressure instantly.

Calories: 66 per serving.
Serves 6 (2½- or 4-quart cooker).
For a 6- or 8-quart cooker, use 1 cup water.

Marmalade Soufflé

4 egg whites
1 tablespoon lemon juice
1 tablespoon sugar
3 tablespoons orange marmalade

1. Beat egg whites until foamy. Beat in lemon juice and sugar; beat until stiff.
2. Fold in orange marmalade.
3. Pour soufflé mixture into four 6-ounce custard cups. Cover each cup with a tent of foil and poke a hole in the foil.
4. Pour 1 cup water into cooker. Place custard cups on rack in cooker.
5. Cover, set control at 5 and place over high heat until control jiggles. Reduce heat and cook 5 minutes (or cook at 15 for 3 minutes).
6. Run cold water over the cooker to reduce pressure instantly. Serve at once.

Calories: 68 per serving.
Serves 4 (6- or 8-quart cooker).
For a 2½- or 4-quart cooker, pressure-cook 2 soufflés at a time.

"Baked" Apples with Orange Sauce

4 medium tart baking apples
1 medium banana
1 tablespoon chopped walnuts
2 teaspoons lemon juice
1 tablespoon brown sugar
  Pinch of salt
  Pinch of nutmeg
⅔ cup orange juice

1. Core apples without piercing blossom end.
2. Mash banana and combine with nuts, lemon juice, brown sugar, salt and nutmeg. Fill apples with this mixture. Place on heatproof dish.
3. Pour orange juice into cooker. Place dish on rack in cooker.
4. Cover, set control at 5 and place over high heat until control jiggles. Reduce heat and cook 4 minutes (or cook at 15 for 2 minutes).
5. Run cold water over the cooker to reduce pressure instantly.
6. Remove apples to a serving plate. If desired, remove rack and thicken sauce by cooking over high heat for a few minutes. Pour sauce over apples.

Calories: 162 per serving.
Serves 4 (2½- to 8-quart cooker).

Stewed Peaches

1 pound ripe peaches
  Cloves
¾ cup water
2 tablespoons sugar
  Juice of ½ lemon
1 cinnamon stick

1. Dip peaches into boiling water, then into cold water. Slip off skins. Cut fruit in half and reserve stones. Stud each peach half with a clove.
2. Heat ¾ cup water in cooker with sugar, lemon juice and cinnamon stick, stirring over low heat until sugar dissolves. Add peaches and peach stones.
3. Cover, set control at 15 and place over high heat until control jiggles. Remove from heat at once.
4. Run cold water over the cooker to reduce pressure instantly.
5. Transfer fruit to a serving bowl. Boil syrup rapidly, uncovered, to thicken. Strain syrup, discarding stones; pour syrup over peaches. Serve warm or chilled.

Calories: 68 per serving.
Serves 4 (2½- to 8-quart cooker.)

Dieter's Rice Pudding

2 egg whites
1 teaspoon vanilla
  Pinch of salt
½ cup nonfat dry milk solids
1 cup cooked rice
2 tablespoons raisins, chopped
½ teaspoon cinnamon
¼ cup water

1. Beat egg whites with vanilla and salt until stiff. Fold in dry milk solids to make a meringue-like mixture.
2. Combine rice, raisins, cinnamon and water; fold in meringue.
3. Grease four 6-ounce custard cups and fill with rice mixture.
4. Pour 1 cup water into cooker. Place custard cups on rack in cooker.
5. Cover, set control at 15 and place over high heat until control jiggles. Reduce heat and cook 15 minutes (or cook at 5 for 22 minutes).
6. Remove from heat and let cool 5 minutes; then run cold water over the cooker to finish reducing pressure.

Calories: 84 per serving.
Serves 4 (6- or 8-quart cooker).
For a 2½- or 4-quart cooker, pressure-cook 2 custard cups at a time.

COOKING
FOR A CROWD

Crowds mean fun. And, thanks to pressure cooking techniques, they can even mean fun for the cook. No need to lock yourself into the kitchen for days in advance. No need to resort to your one tried-and-true quantity casserole.

On the following pages you'll find a wide array of crowd-size pleasers for a variety of occasions. You'll find recipes like Glazed Spareribs and Chicken Roll-Ups to go with drinks at a cocktail party. Or Chicken Paprikash and Jambalaya for the church supper or neighborhood block party. Or, if your plans call for a buffet party at home, consider Curries for a Crowd or Fresh Ham in Beer — to mention but a few.

For quantity recipes like these, a larger cooker — a 12-quart, for example — simplifies preparation and accommodates large amounts of food. And unlike cooking a dish by ordinary heating methods, which take longer to penetrate large quantities of food, a pressure-cooked dish for twenty cooks just as quickly as it does for two. But it does take a larger pot a somewhat longer time to come up to the pressure temperature — so remember to allow for this.

Quantity recipes can also come in handy for do-ahead planning, wherein a single cooking session can take care of two or three meals. Serve one portion to the family, then divide the leftovers into meal-size packages; wrap, label and freeze. You'll always have a dinner on hand.

tip

A recipe planned for a 12-quart cooker can be used in 16- and 22-quart cookers. Remember, big cookers take somewhat longer to reach pressure temperatures — so be sure to allow for this extra time.

Glazed Spareribs

½ cup dark brown sugar
¼ cup vinegar
   Juice of ½ lemon
2 tablespoons tomato paste
1 cup water or dry white wine
3 cloves garlic, minced
1 small onion, minced
½ teaspoon salt
¼ teaspoon oregano
   Pinch of pepper
1 tablespoon Worcestershire sauce
2½ pounds lean spareribs, cut into
   individual portions

1. Combine brown sugar, vinegar, lemon juice, tomato paste, water, garlic, onion, salt, oregano and pepper in cooker. Stir over low heat until sugar is dissolved. Add Worcestershire sauce and spareribs.
2. Cover, set control at 10 and place over high heat until control jiggles. Reduce heat and cook 15 minutes (or cook at 15 for 12 minutes).
3. Remove from heat and let cool 5 minutes; then run cold water over the cooker to finish reducing pressure.
4. Place spareribs on a broiling pan and cover with pan juices. Broil under moderate heat, turning and basting with sauce, until crisp and glazed to a dark brown.

Serves 12 as an appetizer (4- to 12-quart cooker).

Cider Buffet Loaf

1 precooked smoked pork butt
   (5 pounds)
4 cloves
2 cups seedless raisins
1 quart sweet cider
¼ cup dark brown sugar
3 envelopes unflavored gelatin
¼ cup cold water
1½ tablespoons lemon juice
   Pinch each of cayenne pepper and
   nutmeg
2 cups chopped parsley

1. Cover pork with water and let soak for 15 minutes; drain. Stud pork with cloves.
2. Combine raisins, cider and brown sugar in cooker. Add pork.
3. Cover, set control at 10 and place over high heat until control jiggles. Reduce heat and cook 42 minutes (or cook at 15 for 35 minutes).
4. Remove from heat and let cool 5 minutes; then run cold water over the cooker to finish reducing pressure.
5. Transfer the pork to a cutting board. Moisten gelatin in the cold water and add to cooker with lemon juice, cayenne and nutmeg. Cook, stirring, until gelatin is dissolved.
6. Pour into an 8-cup metal mold or 9x5x3-inch loaf pan; refrigerate until fat congeals on top. Carefully remove fat and discard.
7. Discard cloves from the pork; remove the meat from the bone; trim off fat and gristle. Cut the meat into thin julienne strips.
8. When the gelatin mixture begins to set, stir in the meat and parsley. Chill mold 4 hours, until firmly set.
9. Unmold and cut into thin slices.

Serves 12 as an appetizer (2½- to 8-quart cooker).

Spanish Pork and Cumin Hors d'Oeuvres

2 tablespoons butter or margarine
3 pounds lean boneless pork,
    cut into 1-inch cubes
1 cup dry white wine
2 cloves garlic, minced
2 teaspoons cumin
1 teaspoon salt
¼ teaspoon pepper
    Juice of ½ lemon
2 tablespoons chopped parsley
    or fresh coriander

1. In cooker, heat butter until foaming. Add pork and brown well on all sides. Stir in wine, garlic, cumin and salt.
2. Cover, set control at 10 and place over high heat until control jiggles. Reduce heat and cook 12 minutes (or cook at 15 for 9 minutes).
3. Remove from heat and let cool 5 minutes; then run cold water over the cooker to finish reducing pressure.
4. Remove pork cubes to a heated serving dish and cover to keep warm.
5. Add pepper, lemon juice and 1 tablespoon parsley to sauce. Boil, uncovered, over high heat until sauce thickens. Pour sauce over pork cubes. Sprinkle with remaining parsley. Serve with cocktail picks.

Serves 18 as an appetizer (4- to 8-quart cooker).

Pâté Maison

4 tablespoons butter or margarine
1 medium Spanish onion, minced
4 cloves garlic, minced
¾ pound each finely ground pork,
    pork fat and veal (or substitute
    chicken for veal)
1 tablespoon salt
    Pinch of sugar
1 teaspoon each pepper, thyme and
    marjoram
3 eggs
¼ cup brandy
¾ pound pork liver, cut into ¼-inch
    dice
1 pound sliced bacon

1. In cooker, heat butter until foaming. Add onion and garlic and cook, stirring, until onion is wilted. Remove to a mixing bowl.
2. Add pork, pork fat, veal, salt, sugar, pepper, thyme, marjoram, eggs and brandy. Blend well. Fold in pork liver.
3. Line a 9x5x3-inch metal loaf pan with overlapping slices of bacon, leaving about a 2-inch overhang all around the edge. Spoon pâté into the pan and fold ends of bacon back over the top to cover pâté completely. Cover with foil.
4. Pour 2 cups water into cooker. Place mold on rack in cooker.
5. Cover, set control at 10 and place over high heat until control jiggles. Reduce heat and cook 30 minutes (or cook at 15 for 25 minutes).
6. Remove from heat and let cool 5 minutes; then run cold water over the cooker to finish reducing pressure.
7. Uncover pâté and run under the broiler to brown and crisp bacon. Cover with a weighted plate; cool. Serve cold, cut into slices.

Serves 18 to 20 as an appetizer (12-quart cooker).

Chicken Roll-Ups

6 whole chicken breasts, split,
  boned and skinned
½ teaspoon each salt and pepper
½ teaspoon each garlic powder and
  basil
12 thin slices ham
12 thin slices Swiss cheese
  Juice of 1 lemon
1 teaspoon paprika

1. Place halved breasts between sheets
of waxed paper and pound to flatten.
Season with salt, pepper, garlic powder
and basil.
2. Layer 1 slice of ham and 1 slice of
cheese on each chicken piece. Roll up
and secure with wooden picks. Place
chicken roll-ups in a buttered pie plate.
(They may be stacked in layers.) Drizzle
with lemon juice and sprinkle with
paprika.
3. Pour 2 cups water into cooker. Place
pie plate on rack in cooker.
4. Cover, set control at 10 and place
over high heat until control jiggles.
Reduce heat and cook 15 minutes (or
cook at 15 for 12 minutes).
5. Run cold water over the cooker to
reduce pressure instantly.
6. Chill chicken roll-ups and slice into
¼-inch pinwheels. Cover and refrigerate
until ready to serve.

**Serves 18 as an appetizer (6- to
12-quart cooker).**

Curries for a Crowd

½ cup oil
2 medium onions, minced
6 cooking apples, peeled, cored and
  minced
4 small carrots, minced
½ cup flour
3 tablespoons curry powder
6 cups beef or chicken stock or
  bouillon
2 cups apple juice
4 cloves garlic, minced
3 tablespoons brown sugar
2 tablespoons tomato paste
  Juice of 1 lemon
2 teaspoons salt
¼ teaspoon cayenne pepper
1 teaspoon filé powder (optional)
8 cups cubed cooked beef, chicken
  or lamb

1. Heat oil in cooker. Add onions, apples
and carrots; cook, stirring, until onions
are translucent.
2. Add flour and curry powder and cook,
stirring constantly, about 3 minutes. Be
extremely careful that the curry does not
burn.
3. Add remaining ingredients in order
listed and stir well to blend.
4. Cover, set control at 15 and place
over high heat until control jiggles.
Reduce heat and cook 25 minutes (or
cook at 10 for 30 minutes).
5. Remove from heat and let cool 5
minutes; then run cold water over the
cooker to finish reducing pressure.
6. Serve with rice, chutneys (page 86)
and traditional accompaniments: raisins,
salted peanuts, shredded coconut,
chopped onions, chopped cucumbers,
chopped green peppers, sliced bananas
and Bombay duck.

Serves 16 to 18 (12-quart cooker).

NOTE:
Because of their tendency to froth,
apples are not recommended for
pressure-cooking — but they can be
prepared successfully in this recipe.

New England Boiled Dinner Plus

6 to 8 pounds corned beef brisket, well trimmed
8 small white turnips, peeled and cut in half
8 stalks celery, cut into 4-inch pieces
8 medium carrots, quartered
8 potatoes, peeled and cut in half
1 medium cabbage, cored and cut into 16 wedges
3 cups chicken stock or bouillon
1 tablespoon grated horseradish
  Pinch of sugar
1 tablespoon Dijon mustard

1. Place brisket in cooker; add water to cover.
2. Cover, set control at 10 and place over high heat until control jiggles. Reduce heat and cook 40 minutes (or cook at 15 for 30 minutes).
3. Run cold water over the cooker to reduce pressure instantly.
4. Discard liquid and remove brisket.
5. On rack in cooker, place turnips, celery, carrots and potatoes. Place the parboiled brisket on the vegetables and top with cabbage wedges.
6. Combine chicken stock, horseradish, sugar and mustard. Pour over vegetables.
7. Cover, set control at 10 and place over high heat until control jiggles. Reduce heat and cook 10 minutes (or cook at 15 for 8 minutes).
8. Remove from heat and let cool 5 minutes; then run cold water over the cooker to finish reducing pressure.
9. Arrange meat and vegetables on a warm serving platter. Thicken sauce, if desired, by boiling rapidly, uncovered. Season to taste with salt and pepper. Pour sauce over meat and vegetables.

Serves 16 (12-quart cooker).

NOTE:
Cooking time given here is suitable for a square-cut brisket. A thicker cut of the same weight may take 5 or 10 minutes longer to cook.

Cabbage Rolls

1 large head white cabbage
2 cups cooked rice
1 pound ground beef
1 pound sausage meat, crumbled
2 eggs
4 green peppers, seeded and minced
1 large Spanish onion, minced
3 cloves garlic, minced
¼ teaspoon salt
  Pinch each of cumin, cinnamon and pepper
2 cups tomato juice
1 cup beef stock or bouillon
1 can (6 ounces) tomato paste

1. Blanch the whole cabbage in boiling salted water to soften the leaves. Cool under cold running water. Remove leaves and drain. (You will need about 12 large leaves.)
2. Combine rice with ground beef, sausage meat, eggs, vegetables and seasonings.
3. Spoon ¼ cup of meat mixture onto the bottom edge of each cabbage leaf. Turn sides in and roll up, jelly-roll fashion.
4. Pour tomato juice and stock into cooker. Place cabbage rolls, seam side down, on rack in cooker. (They may be stacked in layers.)
5. Cover, set control at 5 and place over high heat until control jiggles. Reduce heat and cook 10 minutes (or cook at 15 for 5 minutes).
6. Remove from heat and let cool 5 minutes; then run cold water over the cooker to finish reducing pressure.
7. Arrange cabbage rolls on a heated serving platter. Remove rack and stir tomato paste into liquid in cooker. Boil rapidly, uncovered, until sauce thickens. Season to taste with sugar and more salt and pepper. Pour over cabbage.

Serves 12 (12-quart cooker).

tip

You can double (or triple) many recipes planned for a 6- or 8-quart cooker and use them in a larger cooker. Just be sure the cooker is no more than ¾ full and that there is enough liquid so that the cooker does not go dry. (The extra liquid is necessary because of the larger diameter and capacity of the big cookers.) Here are some good crowd-pleasers: Boston Baked Beans (p. 27), Blanquette de Veau (p. 40), Boeuf Bourguignonne (p. 39), Lamb Curry (p. 41).

menu idea

Eggplant Caviar (p. 78)

Vegetable Relishes

*Chilled Stuffed Breast
of Veal (this page)*

Cranberry Sauce

Spinach Salad

*Chilled Sliced Oranges
and Berries with Kirsch*

Light Fruitcake (p. 100)

Stuffed Breast of Veal

3 pounds boneless breast of veal
1 teaspoon salt
¼ teaspoon white pepper
½ pound lean ground veal
¼ pound ground smoked ham
1 tablespoon flour
Juice of ½ lemon
1 clove garlic, minced
1 small onion, minced
½ cup minced parsley
3 tablespoons butter or margarine
1 cup chicken stock or bouillon
½ cup dry white wine
½ cup heavy cream

1. Season breast of veal with salt and pepper. Cover and set aside.
2. To prepare stuffing, mix ground veal, ham, flour, lemon juice, garlic, onion and parsley; season with a pinch of salt and pepper.
3. Spread stuffing on the breast of veal.
4. Roll meat jelly-roll fashion and tie with twine at 2-inch intervals.
5. In cooker, heat butter until foamy; brown veal roll on all sides. Add stock and wine.
6. Cover, set control at 10 and place over high heat until control jiggles. Reduce heat and cook 45 minutes (or cook at 15 for 35 minutes).
7. Remove from heat and let cool 5 minutes; then run cold water over the cooker to finish reducing pressure.
8. Transfer veal to a heated serving platter. Remove strings and cover meat with foil to keep it warm while preparing sauce.
9. Add cream to the cooker and cook over high heat, uncovered, until sauce thickens. Adjust seasoning.
10. Cut veal into thin slices; spoon sauce over.

Serves 8 to 10 (6- or 8-quart cooker).

NOTE:
For a cold buffet, serve the stuffed breast of veal chilled, cut into very thin slices; garnish with cranberry sauce.

Choucroute Garni

2 large onions, peeled and quartered
8 cloves
16 thick slices bacon
2 quarts sauerkraut, rinsed and drained
8 smoked loin pork chops, cut into 1-inch cubes
8 thick pork sausages, cut in half
8 knockwurst, cut in half
2 cups chicken stock or bouillon
1 cup dry white wine
1 tablespoon caraway seed
2 bay leaves
4 cloves garlic, peeled
8 potatoes, peeled and cut in half

1. Stud each onion quarter with a clove. Reserve.
2. Line the bottom of cooker with half the bacon. Spread with half the sauerkraut. Cover with smoked pork cubes and half the remaining sauerkraut.
3. Add studded onions, sausages, knockwurst and remaining sauerkraut. Add stock, wine, caraway seed, bay leaves, garlic and potatoes. Top with remaining bacon.
4. Cover, set control at 10 and place over high heat until control jiggles. Reduce heat and cook 42 minutes (or cook at 15 for 35 minutes).
5. Remove from heat and let cool 5 minutes; then run cold water over the cooker to finish reducing pressure.
6. Spoon onto a warm serving platter; serve with Düsseldorf or Dijon mustard.

Serves 16 (6- to 12-quart cooker).

Fresh Ham in Beer

1 fresh ham (10 to 12 pounds)
2 tablespoons salt
1 teaspoon pepper
1 large onion, peeled
3 cloves
1 stalk celery
2 medium carrots, scraped
2 cloves garlic
3 cups beer
¼ cup butter or margarine

1. Remove the outer skin from ham and rub the surface with salt and pepper.
2. Stud the onion with the cloves.
3. Add the ham, the cloved onion and remaining ingredients to the cooker.
4. Cover, set control at 10 and place over high heat until control jiggles. Reduce heat and cook 2 hours and 20 minutes (or cook at 15 for 2 hours).
5. Remove from heat and let stand 5 minutes; then run cold water over the cooker to finish reducing pressure.
6. If desired, transfer ham to a heatproof platter and run under the broiler to glaze. Serve hot or cold.

Serves 16 (12-quart cooker).

NOTE:
Cooked fresh ham may look pink in the center, even when done. A meat thermometer will register 170°.

Duck en Casserole

3 ducklings (about 5 pounds each),
   each cut into 8 pieces
  Flour, salt and pepper
4 cups chicken stock or bouillon
3 cups fresh mushrooms
3 onions, thinly sliced
3 cloves garlic, crushed
  Chopped fresh mint

1. Dredge duckling pieces with flour mixed with salt and pepper.
2. Pour stock into cooker. Arrange duckling pieces on rack in cooker; cover with mushrooms, onions and garlic.
3. Cover, set control at 10 and place over high heat until control jiggles. Reduce heat and cook 35 minutes (or cook at 15 for 30 minutes).
4. Remove from heat and let cool 5 minutes; then run cold water over the cooker to finish reducing pressure.
5. Transfer duckling pieces and vegetables to a serving dish; sprinkle with mint. (If you prefer to crisp the skin of the duckling, place pieces in heatproof casserole and run under the broiler to brown. Transfer to serving dish.)

Serves 12 (12-quart cooker).

Chicken Mole

½ cup oil
3 broiler-fryer chickens, cut into
   serving pieces
4 green peppers, seeded and
   coarsely chopped
2 medium onions, coarsely chopped
6 cloves garlic, minced
6 cups canned or fresh tomato
   sauce (see page 123)
2 tablespoons chili powder
2 teaspoons salt
½ teaspoon Tabasco sauce
4 cloves
2 ounces unsweetened chocolate

1. Heat oil in cooker and brown chicken pieces on all sides. Remove and drain.
2. Add peppers, onions and garlic to the hot oil and cook, stirring, until onions are translucent.
3. Add remaining ingredients in order listed. Return chicken to cooker. Heat, uncovered, just until chocolate is melted.
4. Cover, set control at 10 and place over high heat until control jiggles. Reduce heat and cook 15 minutes (or cook at 15 for 12 minutes).
5. Remove from heat and let cool 5 minutes; then run cold water over the cooker to finish reducing pressure.
6. Serve with rice, refried beans or guacamole salad.

Serves 12 to 14 (12-quart cooker).

Chicken Paprikash with Spätzle

2¼ cups sifted flour
1 egg, beaten
⅔ cup water
½ teaspoon salt
½ cup oil
3 broiler-fryer chickens, cut into serving pieces
3 medium onions, minced
2 green peppers, seeded and minced
3 tablespoons paprika (preferably Hungarian)
2 cups chicken stock or bouillon
1 teaspoon salt
¼ teaspoon white pepper
2 cups dairy sour cream

1. Combine flour, egg, water and ½ teaspoon salt; let stand, covered, 30 minutes.
2. Meanwhile, heat oil in the cooker and brown chicken pieces on all sides. Remove and drain.
3. Add onions and peppers to oil in cooker and cook, stirring, until onions are translucent.
4. Add paprika and cook, stirring, about 1 minute more. Be careful that the spice does not burn.
5. Return the chicken pieces to cooker along with the stock, 1 teaspoon salt and white pepper.
6. Cover, set control at 10 and place over high heat until control jiggles. Reduce heat and cook 15 minutes (or cook at 15 for 12 minutes).
7. Remove from heat and let cool 5 minutes; then run cold water over the cooker to finish reducing pressure.
8. Transfer chicken pieces to a heated serving platter and cover to keep warm. Bring the broth in cooker back to a simmer. Drop spoonfuls of spätzle mixture into the broth and simmer until they float to the surface. With a slotted spoon, transfer spätzle to the platter.
9. Turn off heat and stir the sour cream into the hot broth. Pour over the chicken pieces and spätzle.

Serves 12 to 14 (8- or 12-quart cooker).

Jambalaya

1 cup bacon fat, butter or margarine
3 medium onions, coarsely chopped
4 green peppers, seeded and thinly sliced
3 cups diced cooked ham
2 tablespoons chili powder
1 teaspoon filé powder (optional)
½ teaspoon saffron threads
2 teaspoons salt
½ teaspoon pepper
½ teaspoon cayenne pepper
2 cans (29 ounces each) whole peeled tomatoes
4 cups regular rice
2 pounds raw shrimp, peeled and deveined

1. Heat fat in cooker. Add onions, green peppers and ham. Cook, stirring, until onions are translucent.
2. Sprinkle with seasonings and cook, stirring, about 1 minute more. Be extremely careful that the seasonings do not burn.
3. Drain tomatoes and measure juice. Add enough water to make 8 cups liquid; stir into cooker with tomatoes and rice.
4. Cover, set control at 5 and place over high heat until control jiggles. Reduce heat and cook 10 minutes (or cook at 15 for 7 minutes).
5. Run cold water over the cooker to reduce pressure instantly.
6. Stir in shrimp and cook, uncovered, about 2 minutes, until shrimp are opaque.

Serves 16 (12-quart cooker).

tip

Filé powder, which is made from the leaves of the sassafras tree, is a seasoning traditionally used in Creole dishes. Eighteenth-century settlers along the Gulf Coast learned about the merits of the ground dried sassafras leaf from the local Choctaw Indians and began incorporating its flavoring and thickening powers into their own cooking.

VEGETABLES
WITH A DIFFERENCE

European cooks have long considered the use of the pressure cooker as the best way to maintain the nutrients, flavors and bright colors of vegetables. Thus, it's surprising that American cooks, who are generally so quick to pick up on helpful kitchen equipment, are just now rediscovering the many advantages associated with cooking vegetables in a pressure cooker.

As vegetables and vegetarian meals increase in popularity, another pressure cooker plus comes to the fore: Provided the recommended cooking times are the same, you can cook a number of different vegetables in the same cooker without any mingling of flavors. Unlike water, steam will not transfer flavors nor leach colors.

From Asparagus Vinaigrette to Zucchini Casserole, the recipes on the following pages offer a range of choices that are sure to suit your menu needs. And whether you prepare your vegetables fresh from the garden or fresh from the freezer, you'll find that pressure cooking helps to retain top quality while it cuts the cooking time.

Asparagus Vinaigrette

2 pounds asparagus
2 tablespoons lemon juice
¾ cup oil
¼ cup vinegar
¼ teaspoon salt
Pinch of pepper

1. Snap off tough ends from asparagus and discard. Wash stalks and place on a rectangle of foil, bringing ends of foil up to form "handles." (Do not wrap.)
2. Pour 1 cup water into cooker. Place asparagus on rack in cooker.
3. Cover, set control at 15 and place over high heat until control jiggles. Reduce heat and cook 2 to 4 minutes, depending on thickness of stalks.
4. Run cold water over the cooker to reduce pressure instantly.
5. Remove asparagus to a deep serving dish. Mix lemon juice, oil, vinegar, salt and pepper to make vinaigrette dressing; pour over asparagus. Let cool, then chill.

Serves 8 (2½- to 8-quart cooker).

NOTE:
Placing the asparagus stalks on foil makes it easier to remove them from the cooker.

Green Beans and Potatoes

1 pound green or wax beans
3 medium potatoes, peeled
1 can (16 ounces) tomatoes, with liquid
¼ cup water
1 teaspoon mixed Italian seasoning herbs
Pinch of garlic powder

1. Remove ends of beans. Dice potatoes.
2. Combine tomatoes, water, Italian seasoning and garlic powder in cooker. Add beans and potatoes.

3. Cover, set control at 15 and place over high heat until control jiggles. Reduce heat and cook 3 minutes.
4. Run cold water over the cooker to reduce pressure instantly.
5. Season to taste with salt, pepper and a little sugar.

Serves 6 (2½- to 8-quart cooker).

Orange Beets

2 pounds beets
¾ cup water
1 teaspoon salt
¼ teaspoon pepper
1 tablespoon cornstarch
½ cup orange juice
2 tablespoons sugar
1 tablespoon lemon juice
2 tablespoons butter or margarine

1. Scrub beets well and trim off roots and tops. Peel and cut into slices about ½ inch thick.
2. Pour water into cooker. Add beets, salt and pepper.
3. Cover, set control at 15 and place over high heat until control jiggles. Reduce heat and cook 6 minutes.
4. Run cold water over the cooker to reduce pressure instantly.
5. With a slotted spoon, remove beets to a serving dish. Mix cornstarch with a little orange juice; add to beet liquid with sugar, lemon juice and remaining orange juice. Cook over low heat, stirring, until sauce is thickened. Season to taste with more lemon juice or sugar. Add butter. Pour over beets, or reheat beets in orange sauce.

Serves 6 to 8 (2½- to 8-quart cooker).

Broccoli and Mushrooms

1 bunch broccoli
½ cup beef stock or bouillon
1 can (6 ounces) mushroom caps

1. Trim and discard woody portions of broccoli stems. Slit stems of larger stalks, leaving flowers intact. Wash well.
2. Pour stock into cooker. Place broccoli on rack in cooker.
3. Cover, set control at 15 and place over high heat until control jiggles. Reduce heat and cook 2 minutes.
4. Run cold water over the cooker to reduce pressure instantly.
5. Transfer drained broccoli to a platter.
6. Add mushroom liquid to cooker and boil rapidly, uncovered, to reduce to ¼ cup. Add mushrooms and heat through. Pour over broccoli.

Serves 4 (2½- to 8-quart cooker).

Chestnut Sprouts

1 pint Brussels sprouts
2 tablespoons butter or margarine
½ pound chestnuts, cooked
    (page 78) or canned
1 teaspoon salt
¼ teaspoon pepper
    Pinch of nutmeg

1. Trim off wilted leaves and bottoms of sprouts.
2. Pour 1 cup water into cooker. Place sprouts on rack in cooker.
3. Cover, set control at 15 and place over high heat until control jiggles. Reduce heat and cook 2 minutes for crispness, 4 minutes for softer texture.
4. Run cold water over the cooker to reduce pressure instantly.
5. Drain sprouts. Melt butter in saucepan; add chestnuts and toss to heat. Toss with sprouts. Season with salt, pepper and nutmeg.

Serves 4 (2½- to 8-quart cooker).
This recipe can be doubled in a 4- to 8-quart cooker; use 1½ cups water in Step 2.

Creole Cabbage

4 slices bacon, diced
¼ cup chopped onion
2 or 3 apples, diced
2 or 3 tomatoes, fresh or canned,
    quartered
¼ cup water
2 tablespoons cider vinegar
1 teaspoon salt
1 teaspoon sugar
    Pinch of pepper
6 cups coarsely shredded cabbage

1. Brown bacon in cooker with onion. Add remaining ingredients in order listed.
2. Cover, set control at 15 and place over high heat until control jiggles. Reduce heat and cook 3 minutes.
3. Run cold water over the cooker to reduce pressure instantly.

Serves 6 (6- or 8-quart cooker).
For a 2½- or 4-quart cooker, cut the recipe in half except do not change amounts for tomatoes, water and vinegar.

Carrots Vichy

8 medium carrots, sliced
½ cup club soda (or vichy,
    if available)
2 tablespoons butter or margarine
1 teaspoon salt
¼ teaspoon pepper
2 tablespoons chopped parsley

1. Place carrots in cooker; add club soda.
2. Cover, set control at 15 and place over high heat until control jiggles. Reduce heat and cook 2 minutes.
3. Run cold water over the cooker to reduce pressure instantly.
4. Add butter to cooker; boil, uncovered, until liquid is almost evaporated, shaking pan to prevent burning. Add salt and pepper and sprinkle with parsley.

Serves 4 to 6 (2½- or 4-quart cooker).
For a 6- or 8-quart cooker, use 1 cup club soda.

tip

Cooked chestnuts, whole or mashed, can be served in a variety of ways: as a vegetable (particularly good with chicken or turkey); as an anytime snack; or, pureed and sweetened, as a topping for desserts.

Cauliflower

1 medium head cauliflower
1 cup chicken stock or bouillon
Pinch each of salt and white pepper
1 tablespoon cornstarch
2 tablespoons cold water
Paprika

1. Trim leaves from cauliflower; cut off stem and remove core.
2. Pour stock into cooker. Place cauliflower, rounded side up, on rack in cooker. Sprinkle with salt and pepper.
3. Cover, set control at 15 and place over high heat until control jiggles. Reduce heat and cook 4 to 6 minutes, depending on size of cauliflower.
4. Run cold water over the cooker to reduce pressure instantly.
5. Remove cauliflower to a serving platter. Stir cornstarch with cold water to make a paste; add to liquid in cooker and cook, stirring constantly, until sauce is clear. Adjust seasoning to taste. Pour over cauliflower. Sprinkle with paprika.

Serves 6 (2½- to 8-quart cooker).

Cauliflower Polonaise

Cook cauliflower (above); remove to serving platter. Melt ¼ cup butter or margarine in small skillet; add 3 tablespoons dry bread crumbs and brown lightly. Sprinkle on cauliflower.

Cauliflower au Fromage

Cook cauliflower (above); remove to heatproof platter. Brush cauliflower with melted butter or margarine and sprinkle with grated Swiss cheese. Run platter under the broiler until cheese melts. Sprinkle with paprika.

Chestnuts

3 cups chestnuts

1. With a sharp knife, cut an "x" on the flat side of each chestnut.
2. Place chestnuts in cooker with enough water to cover generously.
3. Cover, set control at 15 and place over high heat until control jiggles. Reduce heat and cook 5 minutes.
4. Run cold water over the cooker to reduce pressure instantly.
5. Remove and discard shells and skins. Return chestnuts to cooker with enough fresh water to cover generously.
6. Cover, set control at 15 and place over high heat until control jiggles. Reduce heat and cook 15 minutes.
7. Run cold water over the cooker to reduce pressure instantly.

Makes about 2 cups (2½- to 8-quart cooker).

Eggplant Caviar

1 medium eggplant
1 small onion, grated
½ clove garlic, grated
1 tomato, peeled, seeded and finely chopped
¼ cup oil (approximately)
Juice of ½ lemon
½ teaspoon salt
Pinch of pepper

1. Wash eggplant; cut into ¼-inch slices.
2. Pour 1 cup water into cooker. Place eggplant on rack in cooker.
3. Cover, set control at 15 and place over high heat until control jiggles. Reduce heat and cook 1 minute.
4. Run cold water over the cooker to reduce pressure instantly.
5. Remove eggplant and drain well; peel, then mash or chop. Mix with onion, garlic and tomato. Stir in oil to desired consistency. Add lemon juice, salt and pepper.
6. Serve chilled, as a dip or spread.

Serves 6 (2½- or 4-quart cooker).

Okra Creole

2 pounds okra
2 tablespoons butter or margarine
1 onion, sliced
1 clove garlic, minced
1 can (16 ounces) stewed tomatoes
¼ cup water

1. Wash okra; trim off stem ends and
leave whole.
2. Melt butter in cooker. Add onion and
garlic and cook over moderate heat,
stirring, until onion is translucent. Add
okra, tomatoes and water.
3. Cover, set control at 15 and place over
high heat until control jiggles. Reduce
heat and cook 3 minutes.
4. Run cold water over the cooker to
reduce pressure instantly.
5. Season to taste with salt, pepper and a
little sugar.

Serves 6 (2½- to 8-quart cooker).

Creamed White Onions, Williamsburg

1 pound small whole white onions
¾ cup water
4 cloves
½ teaspoon salt
   Pinch of white pepper
⅔ cup milk
½ tablespoon butter or margarine
½ tablespoon flour
½ cup chopped peanuts

1. Peel onions, beginning from a
cross-cut at the root end so blossom
end remains intact.
2. Place onions in cooker; add water,
cloves, salt and pepper.
3. Cover, set control at 15 and place over
high heat until control jiggles. Reduce
heat and cook 5 minutes.
4. Run cold water over the cooker to
reduce pressure instantly.
5. With a slotted spoon, transfer onions
to a heated serving dish. Remove
cloves.

6. Bring liquid in cooker to a boil; boil
rapidly to reduce it to about ⅓ cup, then
add milk. Mix butter and flour together to
make a paste and stir into the liquid bit by
bit. Cook, stirring, until sauce is
thickened. Pour sauce over onions and
sprinkle with chopped peanuts.

Serves 4 (2½- or 4-quart cooker).
For a 6- or 8-quart cooker, use 1½ cups
water. Or double the recipe.

Glazed Parsnips

8 medium parsnips
3 tablespoons butter or margarine
3 tablespoons currant jelly or orange
   marmalade
1 teaspoon salt
¼ teaspoon pepper

1. Peel parsnips and cut in half
lengthwise.
2. Pour 1 cup water into cooker. Place
parsnips on rack in cooker.
3. Cover, set control at 15 and place over
high heat until control jiggles. Reduce
heat and cook 7 minutes.
4. Run cold water over the cooker to
reduce pressure instantly.
5. Drain off water. Remove rack but leave
parsnips in cooker. Add butter, jelly, salt
and pepper. Simmer over low heat,
stirring frequently, until parsnips are
coated and glazed.

Serves 6 to 8 (2½- or 4-quart cooker).
For a 6- or 8-quart cooker, use 1½ cups
water in Step 2.

NOTE:
The rack is used in this recipe to keep
the parsnips from getting mushy.

"Baked" Potatoes

4 medium baking potatoes

1. Choose uniform baking potatoes, about 4 to a pound.
2. Scrub potatoes and peel a strip around middle of each; wrap each tightly in foil.
3. Pour 1½ cups water into cooker. Place potatoes on rack in cooker.
4. Cover, set control at 15 and place over high heat until control jiggles. Reduce heat and cook 15 to 20 minutes.
5. Run cold water over the cooker to reduce pressure instantly.
6. Serve in the foil, with salt, pepper and butter or dairy sour cream if desired.

Serves 4 (2½- to 8-quart cooker).
This recipe can be doubled in a 6- or 8-quart cooker; retain 1½ cups water in Step 3.

NOTE:
If desired, potatoes may be cooked without the foil wrapping and then placed in a very hot oven (450° F) for about 10 minutes to dry and crisp the skins.

Scalloped Potatoes

6 potatoes, peeled
3 tablespoons butter or margarine
¼ cup chopped onion
2 tablespoons chopped green pepper
3 tablespoons flour
1 teaspoon salt
¼ teaspoon pepper
¾ cup milk
2 cups grated cheddar cheese
Paprika

1. Cut potatoes into thin slices; reserve.
2. Melt butter in a saucepan; cook onion and green pepper until soft.
3. Remove pan from heat; stir in flour, salt and pepper. Add milk and stir until blended.
4. In a 1-quart heatproof mold, alternate layers of potatoes, sauce, cheese and a sprinkling of paprika, ending with cheese and paprika. Cover mold with foil.

5. Pour 1½ cups water into cooker. Place mold on rack in cooker.
6. Cover, set control at 15 and place over high heat until control jiggles. Reduce heat and cook 10 minutes.
7. Remove from heat and let cool 5 minutes; then run cold water over the cooker to finish reducing pressure. If desired, brown topping quickly by running the mold under the broiler.

Serves 4 to 6 (2½- to 8-quart cooker).

Sweet Potato Casserole

4 medium sweet potatoes, peeled and quartered
1 can (8 ounces) crushed pineapple
1 teaspoon salt
½ teaspoon each pepper, cinnamon and ground cloves
4 tablespoons brown sugar (approximately)
2 tablespoons butter or margarine

1. Pour 1 cup water into cooker. Place sweet potatoes on rack in cooker.
2. Cover, set control at 15 and place over high heat until control jiggles. Reduce heat and cook 6 minutes.
3. Run cold water over the cooker to reduce pressure instantly.
4. Drain potatoes and slice. Arrange in layers in 1-quart heatproof baking dish, alternating with layers of pineapple. Sprinkle each pineapple layer with salt, pepper, cinnamon, cloves and brown sugar. End with brown sugar. Top with butter.
5. To caramelize topping, run baking dish under the broiler for 2 to 3 minutes.

Serves 4 (2½- or 4-quart cooker).
For a 6- or 8-quart cooker, use 1½ cups water in Step 1. Or double the recipe, using 1½ cups water in Step 1.

Spinach Timbales

1 package (10 ounces) frozen
    chopped spinach, thawed
½ onion, grated
⅓ cup dry bread crumbs
1 egg
1 cup milk
¼ cup grated Parmesan cheese
½ teaspoon salt
    Pinch of pepper
    Dash of Worcestershire sauce

1. Squeeze thawed spinach in a cloth
and discard liquid.
2. Combine spinach with remaining
ingredients. Divide among 4 buttered
and lightly floured 6-ounce custard cups.
3. Pour 1½ cups water into cooker.
Place custard cups on rack in cooker.
4. Cover, set control at 15 and place
over high heat until control jiggles.
Reduce heat and cook 3 minutes.
5. Run cold water over the cooker to
reduce pressure instantly. Unmold
timbales on serving platter.

Serves 4 (6- or 8-quart cooker).
For a 2½- or 4-quart cooker, pressure-
cook 2 timbales at a time; use 1 cup
water in Step 3. Or cut the recipe in half,
using 1 cup water in Step 3.

Stuffed Summer Squash

3 medium summer squash
1 tablespoon oil
½ cup chopped green pepper
½ cup chopped onion
2 cloves garlic, chopped
1 pound ground beef
1 cup cooked rice
1 cup tomato sauce
2 eggs
1 teaspoon oregano
1 teaspoon salt
½ teaspoon marjoram
¼ teaspoon pepper

1. Wash squash well and cut in half
lengthwise. Discard seeds.
Scoop out the pulp from each squash
half, leaving a shell about ⅓ inch thick.
Chop the pulp fine.
2. Heat oil in a skillet. Add pulp, green
pepper, onion and garlic; stir until onion
is translucent.
3. Add beef; stir until beef loses its red
color. Stir in remaining ingredients.
4. Mound filling into squash halves; wrap
each in foil, leaving top open.
5. Pour 1 cup water into cooker. Arrange
stuffed squash packets on rack in
cooker.
6. Cover, set control at 15 and place
over high heat until control jiggles.
Reduce heat and cook 5 minutes.
7. Run cold water over the cooker to
reduce pressure instantly.

Serves 6 (6- or 8-quart cooker).
For a 2½- or 4-quart cooker, cut the
recipe in half; retain 1 cup water in
Step 5.

tip

If cooking frozen
vegetables, don't thaw them
(exception: corn on the
cob). Break the frozen block
into smaller pieces and add
to the cooker with ½ cup
water (for 2½- to 8-quart
sizes). Cook 1 to 3 minutes,
as recommended by the
manufacturer.

Acorn Squash

2 acorn squash
4 tablespoons butter or margarine
4 tablespoons brown sugar
1 teaspoon salt
¼ teaspoon pepper
    Juice of ½ lemon

1. Wash squash; cut in half lengthwise and discard pith and seeds.
2. Fill hollows with butter and brown sugar; season with salt, pepper and lemon juice.
3. Pour 2 cups water into cooker and place squash halves, cut side up, on rack in cooker.
4. Cover, set control at 15 and place over high heat until control jiggles. Reduce heat and cook 6 minutes (or cook at 10 for 8 minutes).
5. Run cold water over the cooker to reduce pressure instantly.

Serves 4 (6- or 8-quart cooker).
For a 2½- or 4-quart cooker, cut the recipe in half; use 1 cup water in Step 3.

NOTE:
The cooking time for acorn squash will vary according to its size and maturity.

Stewed Tomatoes

3 pounds tomatoes, peeled and
    chopped
1 tablespoon oil
1 onion, chopped
3 fresh basil leaves or ¼ teaspoon
    dried

1. Dip tomatoes into scalding water, then dip into cold water. Slip off skins. Chop pulp and reserve.
2. Heat oil in cooker and brown onion lightly. Add tomato pulp and basil.
3. Cover, set control at 15 and place over moderate heat until control jiggles. Remove from heat at once.
4. Run cold water over the cooker to reduce pressure instantly.
5. Thicken stew, if desired, by cooking rapidly, uncovered, for a few minutes. Season to taste with salt, pepper and sugar.

Serves 6 (2½- or 4-quart cooker).
For a 6- or 8-quart cooker, add ½ cup water with the tomato pulp.

Turnip Mountain

1½ pounds yellow turnips or
    rutabagas, peeled and cubed
1½ pounds potatoes, peeled and
    quartered
  4 tablespoons butter or margarine
  2 teaspoons salt
½ teaspoon pepper

1. Pour 1½ cups water into cooker. Put turnips and potatoes on rack in cooker.
2. Cover, set control at 15 and place over high heat until control jiggles. Reduce heat and cook 5 minutes.
3. Run cold water over the cooker to reduce pressure instantly.
4. Drain vegetables and mash. Season with butter, salt and pepper. Add a little cream or milk if desired. Spoon into a "mountain" on hot serving platter.

Serves 6 (6- or 8-quart cooker).
For a 2½- or 4-quart cooker, cut the recipe in half; use 1 cup water in Step 1.

tip

It's easy to drain cooked vegetables or other foods right from the pressure cooker. Just remove the gasket from the cover and close the cooker again. Now just pour off the cooking water. The food can't slip out because the cover is "locked" on.

Zucchini Casserole

3 medium zucchini
2 tablespoons butter or magarine
1 teaspoon garlic powder
¼ cup minced onion
1 teaspoon salt
¼ teaspoon pepper
½ cup dry bread crumbs
1 cup grated cheddar cheese

1. Wash zucchini and slice into rounds.
2. Lightly butter a 1½-quart baking dish that will fit into cooker. Alternate layers of zucchini and remaining ingredients in order listed, ending with bread crumbs topped with cheese.
3. Pour 1½ cups water into cooker. Place baking dish on rack in cooker.
4. Cover, set control at 15 and place over high heat until control jiggles. Reduce heat and cook 8 minutes.
5. Run cold water over the cooker to reduce pressure instantly.
6. Brown under the broiler for 2 minutes if desired.

Serves 4 to 6 (6- or 8-quart cooker).
A 2½- or 4-quart cooker can be used if your baking dish fits; use 1 cup water in Step 3.

Ratatouille

⅓ cup oil
4 onions, chopped
2 cloves garlic, minced
2 green peppers, seeded and cut up
1 medium eggplant, cut up
3 small zucchini, cut into ¼-inch slices
1 can (16 ounces) tomatoes, drained and coarsely chopped
½ teaspoon each basil, oregano and thyme
½ teaspoon salt
½ teaspoon pepper

1. Heat oil in cooker. Add onions, garlic and green peppers; cook, stirring, until onions are translucent. Remove from cooker and reserve.
2. In cooker, brown eggplant and zucchini. Add onion mixture, tomatoes, herbs, salt and pepper.
3. Cover, set control at 15 and place over high heat until control jiggles. Reduce heat and cook 3 minutes.
4. Run cold water over the cooker to reduce pressure instantly.
5. Thicken sauce, if desired, by boiling rapidly, uncovered, for a few minutes. Serve hot or cold.

Serves 8 to 10 (4- to 8-quart cooker).
For a 2½-quart cooker, cut the recipe in half. This recipe can also be doubled in an 8-quart cooker.

Meatless Meat Loaf

¼ cup butter or margarine
¾ cup chopped onion
 2 cloves garlic, minced
½ cup chopped celery
½ cup chopped walnuts
½ cup chopped almonds
 1 cup chopped mushrooms,
    squeezed dry
 1 cup rolled oats
 1 cup chick peas, cooked or
    canned, drained and pureed
½ cup grated zucchini
½ cup chopped parsley
 2 eggs
⅓ cup milk
 2 teaspoons salt
 1 teaspoon pepper
½ teaspoon each thyme and nutmeg
    Pinch of sugar

1. Melt butter in a skillet. Add onion, garlic, celery, nuts and mushrooms; cook, stirring, until onions are soft.
2. Add remaining ingredients and mix well. Spoon into a greased 6-cup metal mold. Cover with foil.
3. Pour 2 cups water into cooker. Place mold on rack in cooker.
4. Cover, set control at 10 and place over high heat until control jiggles. Reduce heat and cook 18 minutes (or cook at 15 for 15 minutes).
5. Remove from heat and let cool 5 minutes; then run cold water over the cooker to finish reducing pressure.
6. Set a weighted plate on loaf and let stand at least 15 minutes before serving. This will make slicing easier.

Serves 8 to 10 (6- or 8-quart cooker).
A 2½- or 4-quart cooker can be used if your mold fits.

Vegetable Platter

¼ cup butter or margarine
½ cup water
¼ cup white wine
 1 small head Savoy cabbage, cut
    into 6 wedges
1½ cups green beans, ends trimmed
1½ cups sliced carrots
 1 medium zucchini, washed and cut
    into thick sticks
 6 stalks broccoli, cut in half
 1 cup fresh mushrooms
 1 cup green peas or Chinese pea
    pods

1. Clarify butter: First, melt butter by placing in a cup set in hot water, then pour off clear liquid and reserve; discard milky sediment.
2. Pour reserved butter, water and wine into cooker.
3. Arrange vegetables in separate mounds on the rack of the cooker, placing cabbage wedges between the mounds. (Or wrap each vegetable in a foil packet, leaving the top open. Place packets on rack in cooker).
4. Cover, set control at 15 and place over high heat until control jiggles. Reduce heat and cook 3 minutes.
5. Run cold water over the cooker to reduce pressure instantly.
6. With a slotted spoon, transfer vegetables to a serving dish. Ladle pan juices over vegetables.

Serves 6 (6- or 8-quart cooker).

NOTE:
If you prefer, cook the cabbage whole and use it as a holder for a bowl of hollandaise sauce, as pictured on the cover.

PRESERVES FOR THAT SPECIAL TOUCH

You can preserve the contents of your purse as well as the fruits of the season when you use your pressure cooker to streamline the long, drawn-out chores usually connected with "putting up." You'll find that the pressure cooker dramatically reduces the softening time required for rinds and pulps. Then simply add sugar and use the cooker as an open kettle for the final "cook down."

The recipes on the following pages have been developed to demonstrate the scope of pressure cooker "put-ups." Watermelon Pickle and tart-sweet chutneys can be used to accent a number of main dishes, and the distinctively flavored marmalades, which can virtually be made all through the year, will add a touch of sunshine to many a bread.

No matter how limited your time, you're sure to be able to work these new-fashioned recipes into your schedule. And you'll be delighted for the doing. Discover the special satisfaction that comes with having a shelf of sparkling preserves ready to perk up meals and snacks. And, remember, when used to fill pretty wineglasses, delicate goblets or small apothecary jars, you'll have a collection of ready-made gifts on hand.

Chutney

2 medium onions, peeled
4 small sweet red peppers, seeded
4 small green peppers, seeded
3 or 4 tomatoes (1 pound), skinned
3 or 4 apples (1 pound), peeled and
  cored
⅔ cup seedless raisins
½ ounce crystallized ginger
1 cup cider vinegar
¾ cup sugar
½ teaspoon salt

1. Coarsely chop vegetables, fruit and ginger. Add to cooker with vinegar, sugar and salt. Stir to dissolve sugar.
2. Cover, set control at 15 and place over high heat until control jiggles. Reduce heat and cook 25 minutes.
3. Remove from heat and let cool 5 minutes; then run cold water over the cooker to finish reducing pressure.
4. Boil rapidly, uncovered, for 10 to 15 minutes, until chutney is thickened. Fill hot sterilized jars and seal.

About eight 8-ounce jars (6- or 8-quart cooker).
For a 2½- or 4-quart cooker, cut the recipe in half.

Apricot and Date Chutney

12 ounces dried apricots
1 pound seedless raisins
½ pound pitted dates
½ pound crystallized ginger
3 cloves garlic
4 tablespoons salt
2½ cups white wine vinegar
1 pound brown sugar

1. In cooker, combine all ingredients except sugar.
2. Cover, set control at 15 and place over high heat until control jiggles. Reduce heat and cook 10 minutes.
3. Remove from heat and let pressure reduce naturally.

4. Add sugar and stir over low heat until sugar is dissolved.
5. Thicken liquid, if necessary, by boiling rapidly, uncovered. Test by pouring a little of the chutney onto a saucer. Draw a spoon through it; if the path remains clear, the chutney is ready. Pour into hot sterilized jars and seal.

Eight 8-ounce jars (2½- to 8-quart cooker).

Red Tomato Chutney

2 pounds ripe tomatoes, peeled,
  seeded and chopped
2 cups cider vinegar
1 cup raisins
¼ pound gingerroot, peeled and
  grated
4 cloves garlic, crushed
2 teaspoons salt
½ teaspoon cayenne pepper
2 cups sugar

1. Combine all ingredients except sugar in the cooker.
2. Cover, set control at 15 and place over high heat until control jiggles. Reduce heat and cook 15 minutes.
3. Run cold water over the cooker to reduce pressure instantly.
4. Add sugar and cook, uncovered, over moderate heat, stirring occasionally, 30 minutes or until chutney is rich and thick.
5. Spoon into hot sterilized jars and seal.

Eight 8-ounce jars (2½- to 8-quart cooker).
This recipe can be doubled in a 6- or 8-quart cooker.

Watermelon Pickle

2½ pounds watermelon rind (from
    about ¼ large watermelon)
2½ cups water
  5 cups sugar
2½ cups vinegar
1½ lemons, sliced, with peel
1½ teaspoons whole allspice
1½ teaspoons whole cloves
  2 sticks cinnamon

1. Peel green skin off watermelon rind
and discard. Cut rind into 1-inch squares
(about 8 cups). Soak overnight in salted
water to cover (use ¼ cup salt for each
cup water).
2. Drain and rinse rind.
3. Pour water into cooker. Add rind.
4. Cover, set control at 15 and place
over high heat until control jiggles.
Reduce heat and cook 10 minutes.
5. Run cold water over the cooker to
reduce pressure instantly.
6. Test for tenderness with a wooden
pick. If not tender, bring to a boil and let
boil, uncovered, a few more minutes.
Remove rind from cooker, drain and
reserve.
7. In cooker, boil remaining ingredients
for 5 minutes.
8. Add watermelon rind. Continue to boil
rapidly, uncovered, until rind is
translucent.
9. Pack into hot sterilized jars and seal.
Let stand 2 to 3 weeks before using.

**Ten 8-ounce jars (6- or 8-quart
cooker).**
For a 2½- or 4-quart cooker, cut the
recipe in half.

Dried Apricot Preserve

1 pound dried apricots
1 quart water
3 pounds sugar
  Juice and grated peel of 1 large
  lemon

1. Put apricots and water in cooker.
2. Cover, set control at 15 and place
over high heat until control jiggles.
Reduce heat and cook 15 minutes.
3. Run cold water over the cooker to
reduce pressure instantly.
4. When mixture is cool, puree in a
blender or chop. Return to cooker.
5. Add sugar, lemon juice and peel. Stir
over moderate heat until sugar
dissolves.
6. Boil rapidly, uncovered, until preserve
is thick and boils noisily. (A candy
thermometer will read 220°F.) Test by
pouring a little of the preserve onto a
saucer. Draw a spoon through it; if the
path remains, the preserve is ready.
7. Pour into hot sterilized jars and seal.

**Six 8-ounce jars (2½- to 8-quart
cooker).**

Dried Peach Preserve

Substitute dried peaches for the
apricots. Add 1 cup slivered or halved
almonds with the other ingredients in
Step 5.

Carrot Marmalade

3 pounds carrots, grated
1½ cups water
6 cups sugar
Juice and grated peel of 6 lemons

1. Put carrots and water in cooker.
2. Cover, set control at 15 and place over high heat until control jiggles. Reduce heat and cook 4 minutes.
3. Run cold water over the cooker to reduce pressure instantly.
4. Puree carrots and liquid in a blender or food mill, or press through a sieve. Return to cooker.
5. Add sugar, lemon juice and peel. Stir over moderate heat until sugar dissolves.
6. Boil rapidly, stirring often, until jelly is thickened. (A candy thermometer will read 220°F.) Test by pouring a little jelly onto a saucer. Draw a spoon through the jelly; if the path remains, the jelly is ready.
7. Pour into hot sterilized jars and seal.

About ten 8-ounce jars (2½- to 8-quart cooker).

Amber Marmalade

3 oranges
1 lemon
1 grapefruit
Sugar

1. Wash fruit. Cut unpeeled oranges and lemon in half; remove seeds and stem ends. Slice very thin or grind fine.
2. Trim the yellow outer peel from the grapefruit and cut into thin strips. Discard the white pith and cut the pulp into small pieces. Combine with oranges and lemon.
3. Measure fruit and add an equal volume of water. Let stand overnight. Pour into cooker.
4. Cover, set control at 15 and place over high heat until control jiggles. Reduce heat and cook 25 minutes.
5. Remove from heat and let cool 5 minutes; then run cold water over the cooker to finish reducing pressure.
6. Pour contents into a bowl; let stand at room temperature overnight.
7. Measure fruit and add 1 cup sugar for each cup fruit. Cook, uncovered, over high heat for 20 minutes or until thick. Pieces of fruit and rind will remain suspended in the liquid.
8. Pour into hot sterilized jars and seal.

Ten 8-ounce jars (6- or 8-quart cooker).
For a 2½- or 4-quart cooker, pressure-cook in 2 batches.

Serve it hot or chilled — Ratatouille (page 83), a something-different side dish.

For a crowd. This page: Spanish Pork and Cumin Hors d'Oeuvres (page 69), Chicken Roll-Ups (page 70).

Above: Pâté Maison (page 69), Jambalaya (page 74), New England Boiled Dinner Plus (page 71).

Boston Baked Beans (page 27) and Commonwealth Brown Bread (page 94) — a traditional duo.

STEAMED BREADS AND PUDDINGS

Yesterday's favorites tailored to today. With this anthology of heart-warming, memory-joggling recipes, you can capture all the old-time satisfaction of making fine-textured, delicately blended loaves and molds without heating the oven or steaming up the kitchen.

There's Walnut Bread and colorful Carrot Pudding for health-food fans. For dessert lovers? Blueberry Slump, classic Apple Dumplings, rich Brownie Pudding and New England Indian Pudding are just a few of the sure-to-please choices. And just think what a special holiday gift Dickens' Plum Pudding or Light Fruitcake would make — prepared in a shiny-new mold and elegantly gift-wrapped.

Whatever your taste preferences, whatever your needs, all of these recipes can be steamed to perfection in the security of your pressure cooker.

Commonwealth Brown Bread

¾ cup flour
1 teaspoon baking powder
1 teaspoon baking soda
1 teaspoon salt
1 cup fine dry bread crumbs
3 tablespoons butter or margarine
1 egg
¾ cup buttermilk
½ cup dark molasses

1. Toss flour, baking powder, baking soda and salt to mix. Add bread crumbs and cut in butter.
2. Beat egg well; add buttermilk and molasses. Combine with flour mixture, stirring just until evenly moistened.
3. Fill 4 greased cans (16-ounce size) ⅓ full and cover with a tent of foil to allow for rising.
4. Pour 3 cups water into cooker. Place cans on rack in cooker.
5. Cover, place over heat and allow a small stream of steam to escape from vent tube for 30 minutes. Set control at 5. When control jiggles, reduce heat and cook 30 minutes. (Or allow steam to escape for 30 minutes, then cook at 15 for 20 minutes.)
6. Run cold water over the cooker to reduce pressure instantly.

4 loaves (6- or 8-quart cooker).
For a 4-quart cooker, pressure-cook 2 cans at a time.

Walnut Bread

2½ cups flour
2 teaspoons baking powder
½ teaspoon salt
1 egg
½ cup sugar
1 cup milk
1 cup walnuts, chopped

1. Sift together flour, baking powder and salt; set aside.
2. Beat egg and sugar until light.
3. Add milk and sifted dry ingredients alternately to egg-sugar mixture. Stir in walnuts.
4. Turn into a greased 4-cup metal mold. Cover with foil.
5. Pour 2½ cups water into cooker. Place mold on rack in cooker.
6. Cover, place over heat and allow a small stream of steam to escape from vent tube for 30 minutes. Set control at 5. When control jiggles, reduce heat and cook 30 minutes.
7. Run cold water over the cooker to reduce pressure instantly.

Serves 12 (2½- to 8-quart cooker).

Apple Brown Betty

    3 large tart apples
1½ cups coarse dry bread crumbs
    ⅓ cup brown sugar
    ½ teaspoon salt
        Juice and grated peel of ½ orange
    ⅓ cup butter or margarine, melted
    2 tablespoons brown sugar

1. Peel and slice apples.
2. Combine crumbs with ⅓ cup brown sugar, salt, orange juice and peel.
3. Fill a buttered 6-cup baking dish with alternate layers of apple slices and crumbs. Top with melted butter and cover with foil.
4. Pour 1½ cups water into cooker. Place mold on rack in cooker.
5. Cover, set control at 15 and place over high heat until control jiggles. Reduce heat and cook 15 minutes.
6. Run cold water over the cooker to reduce pressure instantly.
7. Remove dish from cooker. Sprinkle with 2 tablespoons brown sugar and run under the broiler for 3 minutes, until sugar melts and top is brown and crusty.

Serves 6 (6- or 8-quart cooker).
A 2½- or 4-quart cooker can be used if your baking dish fits; use 1 cup water in Step 4.

Apple Dumplings

    2 cups flour
    2 teaspoons baking powder
    ¾ teaspoon salt
    ¼ cup butter or margarine
    ⅔ cup milk
    4 medium baking apples, peeled and cored
    3 tablespoons sugar
    1 tablespoon cinnamon
        Melted butter

1. Toss flour, baking powder and salt to mix. Cut in butter until mixture looks like cornmeal. Add milk and mix to make a soft dough.
2. Roll dough ¼ inch thick into a 12-inch square. Cut into four 6-inch squares.
3. Place an apple in the center of each square. Combine sugar and cinnamon; sprinkle half the mixture over apples. Wrap apples securely in dough, pinching edges to seal.
4. Butter a heatproof plate and arrange dumplings on plate.
5. Pour 2 cups water into cooker. Place plate on rack in cooker.
6. Cover, place over heat and allow a small stream of steam to escape from vent tube for 20 minutes.
7. Run cold water over the cooker until steam no longer escapes from vent tube.
8. Brush cooked dumplings with melted butter and sprinkle with remaining sugar-cinnamon mixture. Run them quickly under the broiler to caramelize the sugar topping.

Serves 4 (6- or 8-quart cooker).
For a 2½- or 4-quart cooker, use 1 cup water in Step 5.

tip

You'll find that a pair of tongs can be very helpful for removing hot food from the cooker. Sometimes two large cooking spoons can also do the trick. To lift the rack (with the food), insert the tines of a long-handled fork into the holes of the rack and lift slowly.

Blueberry Slump

Dumpling Topping (below)
4 cups blueberries
2 cups water
1¾ cups sugar
Pinch of ground cloves
Juice of 1 lemon

1. Prepare Dumpling Topping.
2. Bring blueberries, water and sugar to a boil in cooker; add cloves and lemon juice.
3. Spread topping on boiling blueberry mixture. Simmer uncovered 5 minutes.
4. Cover, place over heat and allow a small stream of steam to escape from vent tube for 15 minutes.
5. Run cold water over the cooker until steam no longer escapes from vent tube. Serve hot.

Serves 6 (2½- or 4-quart cooker).
For a 6- or 8-quart cooker, double the recipe.

Dumpling Topping

1¼ cups flour
1½ teaspoons baking powder
½ teaspoon salt
⅓ cup sugar
¼ cup butter or margarine, softened
1 teaspoon grated lemon peel
⅓ cup milk

1. Toss flour, baking powder, salt and sugar to mix. Cut in butter; add lemon peel.
2. Gently stir in milk to make a soft dough.

Cherry Dumplings

Dumpling Topping for Blueberry Slump (left)
1 can (20 ounces) pitted sour cherries in water
1 tablespoon cornstarch
1 cup sugar
¼ teaspoon ground cloves
2 tablespoons butter or margarine

1. Prepare Dumpling Topping.
2. Drain juice from cherries and measure; add enough water to make 2½ cups. Stir cornstarch with a small amount of this liquid to make a paste. Pour remaining cherry liquid into cooker; add cornstarch paste and bring to a boil, stirring. Add sugar; stir until dissolved.
3. Add cherries, cloves and butter; bring to a boil.
4. Drop dumpling mixture by teaspoons into cooker.
5. Cook 5 minutes, uncovered.
6. Cover, place over heat and allow a small stream of steam to escape from vent tube for 15 minutes.
7. Run cold water over the cooker until steam no longer escapes from vent tube.

Serves 4 (2½- or 4-quart cooker).
For a 6- or 8-quart cooker, double the recipe; measure 5 cups liquid in Step 2.

Cherry Pudding

 4 tablespoons butter or margarine
⅔ cup sugar
 2 eggs, beaten
 1 cup flour
 2 teaspoons baking powder
½ teaspoon salt
¼ teaspoon ground cloves
¼ teaspoon cinnamon
1½ cups canned cherries, pitted and
      cut in half
   Lemon Sauce (below)

1. Cream butter with sugar; add eggs
and beat.
2. Mix flour, baking powder, salt, cloves
and cinnamon. Add to egg mixture.
3. Fold in cherries.
4. Turn into a greased 4-cup metal mold.
Cover with foil.
5. Pour 3 cups water into cooker. Place
mold on rack in cooker.
6. Cover, place over heat and allow
a small stream of steam to escape from
vent tube for 30 minutes. Set control at 5.
When control jiggles, reduce heat and
cook 30 minutes (or cook at 15 for 25
minutes).
7. Run cold water over the cooker to
reduce pressure instantly.
8. Serve pudding with Lemon Sauce.

Serves 6 (2½- to 8-quart cooker).
This recipe can be doubled in a 12-quart
cooker. Use a greased 8-cup metal
mold; retain 3 cups water in Step 5.

Lemon Sauce

½ cup sugar
 1 tablespoon cornstarch
¼ teaspoon salt
 1 cup cold water
 3 tablespoons lemon juice
 1 teaspoon grated lemon peel
 2 tablespoons butter or margarine

1. In a saucepan, mix sugar, cornstarch,
salt and cold water.
2. Bring to a boil and cook, stirring, until
smooth, thickened and clear. Add
remaining ingredients.

Carrot Pudding

⅔ cup flour
⅔ cup sugar
 1 teaspoon baking powder
¾ teaspoon salt
½ teaspoon baking soda
½ teaspoon cinnamon
½ teaspoon ground cloves
 1 cup raisins
 1 cup grated raw carrot
⅓ cup grated raw potato
⅓ cup milk

1. Toss dry ingredients to mix. Stir in
raisins, carrot and potato.
2. Add milk and stir just until dry
ingredients are moistened.
3. Turn into a buttered 4-cup metal
mold. Cover with foil.
4. Pour 3 cups water into cooker. Place
mold on rack in cooker.
5. Cover, place over heat and allow a
small stream of steam to escape for 20
minutes. Set control at 15. When control
jiggles, reduce heat and cook 50
minutes.
6. Run cold water over the cooker to
reduce pressure instantly.

Serves 4 (2½- to 8-quart cooker).

tip

If you prefer to use a metal
mold when a recipe calls for
a baking dish or a heatproof
bowl, reduce the cooking
time by about 20 percent.
Conversely, if you use a glass
baking dish or bowl instead
of a metal mold, allow 20
percent *more* cooking time.

Brownie Pudding

2 tablespoons butter or margarine
½ cup sugar
1 egg
1 cup less 2 tablespoons flour
1 teaspoon baking powder
¼ teaspoon salt
¼ cup cocoa powder
½ cup strong coffee
1 teaspoon vanilla
½ cup chopped nuts

1. Cream butter with sugar; add egg and beat well.
2. Toss flour with baking powder and salt.
3. Stir cocoa powder with coffee to make a smooth paste.
4. Add flour mixture and cocoa paste alternately to butter-egg mixture, ⅓ at a time, blending until smooth after each addition.
5. Stir in vanilla and nuts.
6. Turn into a buttered 4-cup metal mold. Cover with foil.
7. Pour 3 cups water into cooker. Place mold on rack in cooker.
8. Cover, place over heat and allow a small stream of steam to escape from vent tube for 30 minutes. Set control at 5. When control jiggles, reduce heat and cook 30 minutes. (Or allow steam to escape for 30 minutes, then cook at 15 for 18 minutes.)
9. Run cold water over the cooker to reduce pressure instantly.
10. Serve warm, with ice cream or whipped cream if desired.

Serves 4 (2½- to 8-quart cooker).

Bread Pudding

1½ cups cubed dry bread
½ cup sugar
1 teaspoon cinnamon
¼ teaspoon salt
2 cups milk
2 eggs, beaten
1 teaspoon vanilla
½ cup raisins

1. Toss bread cubes with a mixture of sugar, cinnamon and salt.
2. Scald milk and pour over bread. Stir in eggs, vanilla and raisins.
3. Turn mixture into a buttered 4-cup metal mold. Cover with foil.
4. Pour 2 cups water into cooker. Place mold on rack in cooker.
5. Cover, set control at 5 and place over high heat until control jiggles. Reduce heat and cook 25 minutes (or cook at 15 for 15 minutes).
6. Run cold water over the cooker to reduce pressure instantly.
7. If desired, dot with butter and sprinkle with sugar and cinnamon; brown quickly under the broiler.

Serves 6 (2½- to 8-quart cooker).

New England Indian Pudding

3 cups milk
1 cup stone-ground yellow cornmeal
½ cup dark molasses
⅓ cup sugar
1 teaspoon salt
1 teaspoon cinnamon
½ teaspoon ginger

1. Mix 1 cup of the milk with cornmeal.
2. Bring remaining 2 cups milk to a boil in a saucepan; add cornmeal paste and remaining ingredients. Cook, stirring, for 2 minutes.
3. Turn into a buttered 1½-quart baking dish and cover with foil.
4. Pour 1 cup water into cooker. Place mold on rack in cooker.
5. Cover, set control at 15 and place over high heat until control jiggles. Reduce heat and cook 15 minutes.
6. Run cold water over the cooker to reduce pressure instantly.
7. Serve warm, with ice cream or whipped cream if desired.

Serves 6 (6- or 8-quart cooker).
A 2½- or 4-quart cooker can be used if your baking dish fits. Or cut the recipe in half; use a 1-quart baking dish and retain 1 cup water in Step 4.

Date Nut Pudding

2 tablespoons butter or margarine
⅓ cup sugar
1 egg
½ cup flour
1 teaspoon baking powder
½ teaspoon baking soda
½ teaspoon salt
½ teaspoon cinnamon
½ cup chopped pitted dates
½ cup coarsely chopped nuts

1. Cream butter with sugar; add egg and beat well.
2. Toss flour with baking powder, baking soda, salt and cinnamon to mix. Add to butter mixture, beating well.
3. Stir in chopped dates and nuts.
4. Turn into four 6-ounce custard cups (cups should be ½ full). Cover with foil.
5. Pour 2½ cups water into cooker. Place custard cups on rack in cooker.
6. Cover, place over heat and allow a small stream of steam to escape from vent tube for 30 minutes. Set control at 5. When control jiggles, reduce heat and cook 30 minutes. (Or allow steam to escape for 30 minutes, then cook at 15 for 18 minutes.)
7. Run cold water over the cooker to reduce pressure instantly.

Serves 4 (6- or 8-quart cooker).
For a 2½- or 4-quart cooker, pressure-cook 2 custard cups at a time.

tip

Use your pressure cooker to reheat a steamed pudding. Pour 1 cup water into cooker. Return pudding to the mold, cover with foil and place on rack in cooker. Cover, set control at 15 and place over high heat until control jiggles. Remove from heat at once and let pressure reduce naturally.

Dickens' Plum Pudding

¾ cup butter or margarine
½ cup sugar
2 eggs
1 cup flour
1 teaspoon baking powder
1 teaspoon cinnamon
½ teaspoon nutmeg
½ teaspoon ground cloves
½ teaspoon salt
⅓ cup milk
1 cup seedless raisins
½ cup chopped mixed candied fruit
2 tablespoons sugar
2 tablespoons water
2 tablespoons dark rum

1. Cream butter with ½ cup sugar until light. Add eggs, one at a time, beating well after each addition.
2. Toss flour, baking powder, spices and salt to mix. Add to egg mixture alternately with milk, blending well after each addition.
3. Stir in raisins and candied fruit.
4. Turn into a buttered 4-cup metal mold. Cover with foil.
5. Pour 3 cups water into cooker. Place mold on rack in cooker.
6. Cover, place over heat and allow a small stream of steam to escape from vent tube for 20 minutes. Set control at 15. When control jiggles, reduce heat and cook 40 minutes.
7. Run cold water over the cooker to reduce pressure instantly
8. Dissolve 2 tablespoons sugar in the water; add rum. Pierce pudding with a long-tined fork or cake tester and baste with rum sauce. Serve warm.

Serves 8 (2½- to 8-quart cooker).

Light Fruitcake

⅓ cup butter or margarine
⅓ cup sugar
2 eggs
1 cup flour
1 teaspoon baking powder
½ teaspoon salt
3 tablespoons milk
1⅓ cups chopped mixed dried fruit and peel (light colors only)
3 tablespoons rum (optional)

1. Cream butter with sugar. Beat in eggs, one at a time; beat until fluffy.
2. Toss ¾ cup of the flour, the baking powder and salt to mix. Add to butter mixture alternately with milk, blending until smooth after each addition.
3. Toss chopped fruit with remaining ¼ cup flour; stir into batter.
4. Turn into a buttered 4-cup metal ring mold and cover with foil.
5. Pour 3 cups water into cooker. Place mold on rack in cooker.
6. Cover, place over heat and allow a small stream of steam to escape from vent tube for 15 minutes. Set control at 15. When control jiggles, reduce heat and cook 40 minutes.
7. Run cold water over the cooker to reduce pressure instantly.
8. Unmold cake. Pierce with a skewer and moisten with 3 tablespoons rum if desired. Cool before slicing.

Serves 6 to 8 (2½- to 8-quart cooker).

SWEETS AND FANCIES

Imagine a delicate Apricot Soufflé cooked in five minutes. Or an amber-syruped Flan in three minutes. You can cook a perfect caramel, right in the condensed milk can, in minutes instead of hours. Or turn out a Prune Whip that will rival your grandmother's. All of these are possible — with your pressure cooker.

Even fruit specialties like Baked Apples can find a place in your rush-hour repertoire. They can be ready in nine minutes in your pressure cooker as opposed to the usual 45 minutes of oven baking. Similarly, other long-cooking fruits, such as Brandied Pears, Compote of Dried Fruits and Candied Fruit Peel, can be yours without hours of simmering, stewing or soaking.

Whether you're looking for the grand finale for a dinner party menu or a sweet snack for the family, you'll find that desserts of distinction can be yours in minutes.

"Baked" Stuffed Apples

4 large baking apples, about 3
    inches at base
¼ cup brown sugar
½ teaspoon cinnamon
½ teaspoon nutmeg
2 teaspoons butter or margarine
6 tablespoons granulated sugar
¼ cup red wine
    Pinch of salt

1. Wash and core apples; peel top half
only.
2. Fill cavities with a mixture of brown
sugar, cinnamon, nutmeg and butter.
Arrange apples in an 8- or 9-inch pie
pan.
3. Pour 1 cup water into cooker. Place
pie pan on rack in cooker.
4. Sprinkle apples with 2 tablespoons of
the granulated sugar.
5. Cover, set control at 15 and place
over high heat until control jiggles.
Reduce heat and cook 8 minutes.
6. Run cold water over the cooker to
reduce pressure instantly.
7. Remove apples and rack. Add wine,
remaining sugar and salt to cooker; boil
rapidly to thicken. Pour sauce over
baked apples.

Serves 4 (6- or 8-quart cooker).
For a 2½- or 4-quart cooker, pressure-
bake 2 apples at a time (in a smaller
dish). Or cut the recipe in half, retaining
1 cup water in Step 3.

NOTE:
Vary the stuffing for the apples to suit
your own taste: raisins, nuts, dates,
whole cranberry sauce, drained crushed
pineapple all add zest.

"Baked" Bananas

6 small, slightly green bananas
2 tablespoons lemon juice
¼ cup butter or margarine, melted
2 tablespoons brown sugar

1. Peel bananas. Roll in lemon juice,
then in melted butter, then in brown
sugar. Arrange bananas on a heatproof
plate.
2. Pour ½ cup water into cooker. Place
plate on rack in cooker.
3. Cover, set control at 5 and place over
high heat until control jiggles. Reduce
heat and cook 1 minute. (Or set control
at 15 and place over high heat until
control jiggles. Remove from heat at
once.)
4. Run cold water over the cooker to
reduce pressure instantly.

Serves 6 (2½- to 8-quart cooker).

NOTE:
Try this as a "something different"
accompaniment for meat. But don't peel
the bananas and don't add seasonings.
Serve with skins on, to be peeled at the
table. Season with butter, salt and
pepper as you eat.

tip

When looking for good
baking apples, what
varieties should you
choose? Granny Smith,
Greening, Cortland,
Winesap, Northern Spy and
Rome Beauty are all
recommended.

Glazed Peaches

 4 firm, ripe peaches
 ½ cup orange juice
 1 tablespoon lemon juice
 4 tablespoons sugar

1. Dip peaches into boiling water, then into cold water. Slip off skins. Arrange peaches on rack in cooker.
2. Add orange juice and lemon juice to cooker. Sprinkle peaches with sugar.
3. Cover, set control at 15 and place over high heat until control jiggles. Remove from heat at once.
4. Let pressure reduce naturally.
5. Transfer peaches to a heatproof serving dish. Spoon sauce over peaches and place under the broiler to glaze; or serve unglazed.

Serves 4 (2½- or 4-quart cooker).
For a 6- or 8-quart cooker, use 1 cup orange juice, 2 tablespoons lemon juice and ½ cup sugar. Before spooning sauce over fruit, boil rapidly to thicken.

Brandied Peaches

 6 firm, ripe peaches
 ½ cup sugar
 2 tablespoons brandy

1. Dip peaches into boiling water, then into cold water. Slip off skins. Roll top half of each peach in sugar.
2. Pour ¾ cup water into cooker. Place fruit, sugared side up, on rack in cooker.
3. Cover, set control at 15 and place over high heat until control jiggles. Remove from heat at once.
4. Run cold water over the cooker to reduce pressure instantly.
5. With a slotted spoon, transfer peaches to a serving dish. Boil liquid rapidly, uncovered, until syrup is thickened; stir in brandy. Spoon over peaches.

Serves 6 (2½- to 8-quart cooker).

Brandied Pears

 4 firm, barely ripe Bartlett pears
 1 tablespoon sweetened condensed
   milk
 1 tablespoon brandy
   Cinnamon

1. Peel pears. Cut in half lengthwise and remove cores. Arrange hollow side up on a heatproof plate.
2. Mix milk and brandy and fill hollows. Sprinkle with cinnamon. Cover with foil.
3. Pour 1 cup water into cooker. Place plate on rack in cooker.
4. Cover, set control at 15 and place over high heat until control jiggles. Reduce heat and cook 4 minutes.
5. Run cold water over the cooker to reduce pressure instantly.

Serves 4 (2½- to 8-quart cooker).
This recipe can be doubled in a 6- or 8-quart cooker; use 1½ cups water in Step 3.

Pears in Red Wine

 6 firm Bartlett pears
 1 cup red wine
 ¼ lemon, with peel
 1- inch piece cinnamon stick
 ½ cup sugar

1. Peel pears, leaving stems intact. Place in cooker with wine, lemon and cinnamon.
2. Cover, set control at 10 and place over high heat until control jiggles. Remove from heat at once.
3. Run cold water over the cooker to reduce pressure instantly.
4. Test pears for tenderness. If tender, transfer to a dish with a slotted spoon. Add sugar to liquid in cooker; stir to dissolve. Thicken sauce, if desired, by boiling rapidly for a few minutes. Pour over pears. If pears are not as tender as you like, cook them along with the sugar and wine.

Serves 6 (2½- to 8-quart cooker).

Stuffed Pears

4 firm, ripe Bartlett pears, about 2½
   inches at base
¼ cup whole cranberry sauce
¼ cup chopped walnuts

1. Peel pears, leaving stems intact.
Remove each blossom in a small cone;
reserve cone. Scrape out core through
the hole in the bottom of the fruit.
2. Stuff hollows with a mixture of
cranberry sauce and nuts. Use reserved
cone as a cork. Arrange pears, stems up,
on a heatproof plate.
3. Pour ½ cup hot water into cooker.
Place plate on rack in cooker.
4. Cover, set control at 15 and place over
high heat until control jiggles. Reduce
heat and cook 1 minute.
5. Remove from heat and let pressure
reduce naturally.

Serves 4 (2½- or 4-quart cooker).
For a 6- or 8-quart cooker, use ¾ cup
water in Step 3. Or double the recipe,
using 1 cup water in Step 3.

Prune-Plums al Vino

2 pounds Italian prune-plums
½ cup water
½ cup sweet red wine
3 cloves
½ cup sugar

1. Wash prunes and leave whole. Prick a
tiny hole in the round ends. Put prunes in
cooker with water, wine and cloves.
2. Cover, set control at 15 and place over
high heat until control jiggles. Remove
from heat at once.
3. Run cold water over the cooker to
reduce pressure instantly.
4. With a slotted spoon, transfer prunes
to a serving dish. Add sugar to liquid in
cooker; stir to dissolve. Thicken sauce, if
desired, by boiling rapidly, uncovered, for
a few minutes. Pour over prunes.

Serves 8 (2½- to 8-quart cooker).

Spiced Prune Crock

1 pound dried prunes
1½ cups water
½ cup sugar
½ cup vinegar
½ teaspoon grated lemon peel
2 cloves
¼ teaspoon allspice
¼ teaspoon ginger
1 cinnamon stick

1. Place prunes in cooker; add water.
2. Cover, set control at 15 and place over
high heat until control jiggles. Reduce
heat and cook 5 minutes.
3. Run cold water over the cooker to
reduce heat instantly.
4. With a slotted spoon, transfer prunes
to a heatproof serving bowl. Add sugar,
vinegar and remaining ingredients to
liquid in cooker. Stir to dissolve sugar.
Boil rapidly, uncovered, until mixture
becomes a syrup. Pour boiling syrup over
prunes.
5. Cool. Serve spiced prunes as an
accompaniment for meat or poultry, or as
a sauce for cake or ice cream.

**Makes 3 to 4 cups (2½- to 8-quart
cooker).**

Compote
of Dried Fruits

**1 pound (about 2½ cups) dried fruits
 (prunes, peaches, apricots,
 apples)
2 cups water
1 tablespoon cornstarch
½ cup sugar
 Pinch of salt
 Juice and grated peel of 1 lemon**

1. Put your favorite assortment of dried fruits in cooker. Add water.
2. Cover, set control at 15 and place over high heat until control jiggles. Reduce heat and cook 10 minutes.
3. Run cold water over the cooker to reduce pressure instantly.
4. With a slotted spoon, transfer fruit to a serving dish.
5. Mix cornstarch with 1 tablespoon cold water; stir into cooker. Add sugar, salt, lemon juice and peel. Cook, stirring, until sauce is clear and thickened. Pour over fruit.

Serves 6 (2½- to 8-quart cooker).

Apricot Soufflé

**½ package dried apricots (6 ounces)
2 tablespoons sugar
1 cup water
1 tablespoon brandy
3 egg whites**

1. Combine apricots, sugar and water in cooker.
2. Cover, set control at 15 and place over high heat until control jiggles. Reduce heat and cook 10 minutes.
3. Run cold water over the cooker to reduce pressure instantly.
4. If necessary, boil rapidly, uncovered, to reduce liquid almost entirely.
5. Puree fruit in a blender or force through a food mill. Add more sugar if desired. Beat egg whites until stiff; fold in.
6. Turn into 4 buttered 6-ounce custard cups (cups should be ½ full). Cover with a tent of foil and poke a hole in top of foil.
7. Pour 1 cup water into cooker. Place custard cups on rack in cooker.
8. Cover, set control at 5 and place over high heat until control jiggles. Reduce heat and cook 5 minutes (or cook at 15 for 4 minutes).
9. Run cold water over the cooker to reduce pressure instantly. Serve at once.

Serves 4 (6- or 8-quart cooker).
For a 2½- or 4-quart cooker, pressure-cook 2 soufflés at a time.

Prune Whip

½ pound dried prunes (about 1¼
   cups)
1 cup water
¼ cup orange marmalade
1 teaspoon lemon juice
2 egg whites
2 tablespoons sugar
   Grated lemon peel

1. Combine prunes and water in cooker.
2. Cover, set control at 15 and place over high heat until control jiggles. Reduce heat and cook 15 minutes.
3. Run cold water over the cooker to reduce pressure instantly.
4. Drain prunes; stone and mash thoroughly. Add marmalade and lemon juice.
5. Beat egg whites until foamy. Gradually beat in sugar and beat until stiff.
6. Fold in prunes. Pile whip into dessert dishes and sprinkle with lemon peel.

Serves 6 (2½- or 4-quart cooker).
For a 6- or 8-quart cooker, double the recipe.

tip

A 2½- or 4-quart cooker will hold 3 standard-size custard cups. If you are cooking a custard or other "non-rising" recipe, you can expand that capacity by placing another rack (ordered from the manufacturer or improvised) on top of the first layer of custard cups, and then add 2 or 3 more cups.

Flan
(Caramel Custard)

½ cup sugar
2 cups milk
2 eggs, lightly beaten
1 teaspoon vanilla
¼ teaspoon salt

1. Place ¼ cup of the sugar in small, heavy skillet and stir over low heat until sugar melts and is light brown in color.
2. Divide syrup among four 6-ounce custard cups.
3. Meanwhile, in small saucepan bring milk to the boiling point; stir in remaining ¼ cup sugar.
4. Beat ½ cup of the hot milk into eggs; then beat egg mixture into remaining hot milk. Add vanilla and salt. Pour into custard cups over syrup; cover with foil.

5. Pour 1 cup water into cooker. Place custard cups on rack in cooker.
6. Cover, set control at 5 and place over high heat until control jiggles. Reduce heat and cook 3 minutes (or cook at 15 for 1 minute).
7. Remove from heat and let stand 5 minutes; then run cold water over the cooker to finish reducing pressure.

Serves 4 (6- or 8-quart cooker).
For a 2½- or 4-quart cooker, pressure-cook 2 custard cups at a time.

Orange Custard in Orange Cups

4 navel oranges
2 eggs, lightly beaten
2 tablespoons sugar
   Pinch of salt
2 cups hot milk
1 teaspoon brandy
   Pinch of nutmeg
1 teaspoon grated orange peel

1. Cut a ¼-inch slice from the top of each orange. Hollow out the inside and reserve fruit and juice for other use.
2. Combine remaining ingredients. Pour custard into orange shells, filling them to within ½ inch of the top.
3. Pour 1½ cups water into cooker. Place orange shells on rack in cooker.
4. Cover, set control at 5 and place over high heat until control jiggles. Reduce heat and cook 2½ minutes (or cook at 15 for 1 minute).
5. Remove from heat and let cool 5 minutes; then run cold water over the cooker to finish reducing pressure.
6. Garnish with whipped cream if desired.

Serves 4 (6- or 8-quart cooker).
For a 2½- or 4-quart cooker, pressure-cook 2 orange shells at a time.

Mocha Custard

**2 squares unsweetened baking
 chocolate**
2 cups milk
2 teaspoons instant coffee powder
2 eggs
⅓ cup sugar
½ teaspoon salt
1 teaspoon vanilla

1. Cut chocolate into pieces. Add to milk
in saucepan and heat, stirring, until
chocolate is melted.
2. Add instant coffee powder and blend
well with a whisk.
3. Beat eggs; add sugar, salt and
vanilla. Beat ½ cup of the hot chocolate
milk into eggs. Then beat egg mixture
into remaining hot milk. Pour into four
6-ounce custard cups and cover with
foil.
4. Pour 1 cup water into cooker. Place
custard cups on rack in cooker.
5. Cover, set control at 5 and place
over high heat until control jiggles.
Reduce heat and cook 3 minutes (or
cook at 15 for 1 minute).
6. Remove from heat and let cool 5
minutes; then run cold water over the
cooker to finish reducing pressure.
7. Serve chilled.

Serves 4 (6- or 8-quart cooker).
For a 2½- or 4-quart cooker, pressure-
cook 2 custard cups at a time.

Chocolate Custard

Omit coffee powder and decrease sugar
to ¼ cup in the recipe for Mocha
Custard.

Coffee Caramel Pudding

**2 cans (14 ounces each) sweetened
 condensed milk**
1 cup hot coffee

1. Pour 4 cups water into cooker.
Remove labels and place unopened
cans of sweetened condensed milk on
rack in cooker.
2. Cover, set control at 15 and place
over high heat until control jiggles.
Reduce heat and cook 50 minutes.
3. Remove from heat and let pressure
reduce naturally. Let cans cool before
opening, but do not chill.
4. With a rotary beater, beat caramelized
milk with hot coffee until smooth and
well blended.
5. Pour into sherbet glasses and chill.

Serves 8 (2½- or 4-quart cooker).
For a 6- or 8-quart cooker, use 6 cups
water in Step 1.

Caramel Fruit Pie

1. Substitute ⅔ cup pineapple juice for
the coffee in the recipe for Coffee
Caramel Pudding.
2. Fill a baked pie shell with the mixture
and chill. Top with sliced fruit —
bananas, peaches, nectarines or
pineapple. Or, line the pie shell with fruit,
then cover with caramel mixture.
Garnish with whipped cream or chopped
nuts.

Quick Rice Pudding

1 cup very soft cooked white rice
1 egg, beaten
¼ cup sugar
   Pinch of salt
1 teaspoon vanilla
2 cups hot milk

1. Mix all ingredients. Pour into a 4-cup metal mold. Cover with foil.
2. Pour 1 cup water into cooker. Place mold on rack in cooker.
3. Cover, set control at 15 and place over high heat until control jiggles. Reduce heat and cook 15 minutes (or cook at 5 for 22 minutes).
4. Remove from heat and let cool 5 minutes; then run cold water over the cooker to finish reducing pressure.

Serves 4 (2½- or 4-quart cooker).
For a 6- or 8-quart cooker, use 1½ cups water in Step 2.

Butterscotch Fudge

1 can (14 ounces) sweetened
   condensed milk
1 package (12 ounces) butterscotch
   bits
½ cup chopped walnuts
1 teaspoon vanilla

1. Combine milk and butterscotch bits in a 4-cup metal mold. Cover with foil.
2. Pour 2 cups water into cooker. Place mold on rack in cooker.
3. Cover, set control at 15 and place over high heat until control jiggles. Reduce heat and cook 5 minutes.
4. Run cold water over the cooker to reduce pressure instantly.
5. Stir fudge to blend; add nuts and vanilla. Turn into a 9-inch square cake pan. Fudge will harden as it cools. When cool, cut into squares.

Makes about 1½ pounds (2½- to 8-quart cooker).

Candied Fruit Peel

Peel of 3 grapefruit or 6 oranges
1 teaspoon salt
2½ cups sugar
1 cup water

1. Remove yellow or orange part of grapefruit or orange peel, discarding white membrane. Cut colored peel into ¼-inch strips.
2. Place peel and salt in cooker. Add water to level of 2 inches from top of cooker.
3. Cover, set control at 15 and place over high heat until control jiggles. Reduce heat and cook 20 minutes.
4. Run cold water over the cooker to reduce pressure instantly.
5. Drain peel. In cooker, bring sugar and 1 cup water to a boil. Add peel and cook, stirring often, until most of the syrup has been absorbed.
6. With a slotted spoon, transfer peel to a sheet of waxed paper sprinkled with more sugar. Roll to coat. Let dry several hours or overnight. Store in a tightly covered container.

40 to 48 pieces (2½- to 8-quart cooker).

Pleasing "put-ups" — Amber Marmalade (page 88), Chutney (page 86), Watermelon Pickle (page 87).

Make a special Christmas memory for family and friends — Dickens' Plum Pudding (page 100).

Brandied Peaches (page 103), Compote of Dried Fruits (page 105), Pears in Red Wine (page 103).

Garden-fresh flavor all year long — Dilly Beans (page 123) and Zucchini Italian Style (page 122).

CANNING — THE EASY WAY

Canning — there was a time when you had to do it; today, you choose to. And for a variety of reasons. For some, canning is an economical step — to preserve the plentiful in-season foods (whether from your own garden or from a produce stand) for those times of the year when the same products are either unavailable or untouchably expensive. For others, canning is a labor of love and self-expression — to achieve a certainty about the high quality of the product that is virtually impossible to obtain otherwise. For all, canning in a pressure cooker means more than convenience and speed: it is the only method recommended as safe by the U.S. Department of Agriculture for the home preservation of meats, poultry, seafood and vegetables — in other words, all low-acid foods. It is equally smart, if not mandatory, to use the pressure cooker for putting up foods that don't require temperatures above the boiling point, such as fruits and tomatoes, because you can save one-third to one-half the time. And, correspondingly, you save fuel.

But canning is not the occasion for experimentation. The following instructions, charts and recipes, all based on U.S. Department of Agriculture recommendations, should be your guide. To ensure the health and safety of your family and friends, no deviations should be made.

Go ahead. Feast your family with peaches in January, with asparagus in September, with whatever you have on your shelf whenever you choose to serve it. It's a special freedom of choice that canning gives you. And you'll find that canning is a "can-do" thing. It doesn't really call for experience; it simply calls for following instructions. And anyone can do that.

Pressure Canning Directions

The U.S. Department of Agriculture recommends pressure canning as *the only safe way* to can meats, poultry, seafood and most vegetables. Although fruits and acid vegetables like sauerkraut and tomatoes do not require canning under pressure for reasons of safety, it makes good sense to use this method because it saves so much time and energy.

Before you use your pressure cooker for canning, pour 1 quart water and 1 tablespoon vinegar into cooker. Cover, set control at 5 and place over high heat until control jiggles. Reduce heat so that control jiggles 3 to 4 times a minute. Run cold water over the cooker to reduce pressure instantly. Repeat procedure with control set at 10. This will familiarize you with the heat level your range requires to maintain the pressure your recipe calls for. This is important because turning the heat up and down can cause uneven pressure, which forces liquid out of jars. Notice that less heat is needed to maintain 5 pounds pressure than to maintain 10 pounds. (Continued application of high heat when control is set at 5 may prevent it from jiggling properly.)

1. Use only standard jars made for home canning. (They have the manufacturer's name blown in the glass.) Examine jars and lids carefully to see that there are no nicks, cracks or sharp edges.

2. If your jars call for rubber rings, use only brand-new ones. If they call for metal bands and lids, use only brand-new lids, unless lid manufacturer states that they can be reused.

3. It is not necessary to sterilize jars for pressure canning. Do wash jars, caps and rubber rings thoroughly in hot suds. Rinse. Keep jars covered with hot water until filled. Place metal lids and rubber rings in hot or boiling water as directed by manufacturer.

4. Select fresh, firm (not overripe) fruits and vegetables. Wash and prepare food according to chart directions (pages 117–120) or recipes (pages 121–123).

5. Fit on rubber ring if necessary.

6. Pack jars (a jar funnel will make this easier); then fill with syrup, juice or water, allowing recommended headspace between food and the closure, according to chart directions or recipes. If desired, add salt to jars of meat or vegetables.

7. Insert the blade of a table knife around the inside of each jar to release any trapped air bubbles.

8. Wipe rim of jars clean so no seeds, pulp or liquid prevent a good seal. Close lids according to manufacturer's instructions.

9. Place cooker on heating unit and place rack in cooker. Pour in amount of hot water your cooker requires. (See Cooker Canning Capacity, page 115.) Add 1 tablespoon vinegar or 1 teaspoon cream of tartar to help prevent water stains in cooker and on jars.

10. Place jars on rack in cooker. Sides of jars may touch each other.

11. Cover cooker and set control at 5 (228° F), 10 (240° F) or 15 (250° F), according to chart directions or recipes. Turn heat on high. When control jiggles vigorously, start to count processing time. Reduce heat but keep it high enough so that control jiggles 3 to 4 times a minute. Prevent drafts from blowing over cooker. Process for length of time given on charts or in recipes.

12. When processing time is completed, turn off heat. (If using an electric range, remove cooker from heating unit.) Let pressure reduce naturally, about 20 to 25 minutes for a small cooker filled to capacity and about 40 to 45 minutes for a large cooker. Do not set the cooker in water or run water over it.

13. When pressure has reduced naturally, test by nudging control. If no steam spurts out, remove control. Lift off cover, tilting the far side up so that steam escapes away from you. The important test is *seeing* steam. If you see steam spurt out when you nudge the control, the pressure is not down. If you do not see steam, the pressure *is* down and you may remove control. The hissing is air rushing into the cooker, not steam escaping.

14. Using a jar lifter, remove jars from cooker and set *upright* on a cooling rack or several thicknesses of cloth (not on a cold surface). Keep jars out of drafts. Complete seal if jars are not self-sealing. (See How to Close Jars, page 116.) If any liquid boiled out during processing, it is all right to seal jar as it is. Fruits and vegetables not covered with liquid may turn a darker color, but they will not spoil if they have been processed at the right pressure for the right time and if the lid is sealed.

15. After 12 hours, remove screw bands from jars that have metal lids. If the screw band is difficult to remove, cover with a hot, damp cloth for a minute and try again. Do not force off screw bands because this may break the seal.

16. Examine jars for leaks. To test seal of metal lid, tap with a teaspoon. A clear ring is a sign of a good seal. If lid is curved down and does not move when pressed, that is also a sign of a good seal. If jar leaks, use contents at once or reprocess with new lid for full recommended processing time.

17. Wipe jars with damp cloth. Dry and label with contents and date. Store in cool, dry place.

18. Never taste food you think may have spoiled: destroy it. A leaking jar or a bulged lid may be a sign of spoilage, so don't take chances.

tip

The 16-quart cooker can hold two layers of half-pint jars. Place rack in bottom of cooker. Place jars on rack. Then place a flat, perforated tray or trivet on top of jars and add second tier of jars. The 22-quart cooker can hold two layers of pint jars or three of half-pints and comes equipped with two racks.

Cooker Canning Capacity

SIZE OF COOKER	Half-Pints	Pints Regular	Pints Wide Mouth	Quarts	Amount of Water for Processing at Full Capacity*
2½-Quart	5	—	—	—	1 Quart
4-Quart	5	4	3	—	1 Quart
6-Quart	8	7	5	—	1½ Quarts
8-Quart	8	7	5	4	1½ Quarts
12-Quart	13	10	8	7	2 Quarts
16-Quart	26**	10	8	7	2 Quarts
22-Quart***	38**	20**	16**	7	2 Quarts

*If processing at less than full capacity in any size cooker, add an extra pint of water.

**Jars are stacked in layers.

***If may take up to an hour before control jiggles.

Note: To any size cooker, add 1 tablespoon vinegar or 1 teaspoon cream of tartar with the water.

How to Close Jars

The illustrations below show the traditional jar closures. Recently other lids, using newly developed materials and designs, have appeared on the market. It is *very important* to pretreat and use all lids strictly according to manufacturer's directions.

A flat metal lid with sealing compound and a metal screw band, which fits a standard mason jar.

1. After filling jar, wipe rim clean.
2. Place new lid in hot or boiling water, according to manufacturer's directions.
3. Put lid on jar with sealing compound next to glass.
4. Screw metal band on tightly by hand. Do not use a wrench.
5. This jar is self-sealing. Do not tighten after jar is processed and removed from cooker.

A porcelain-lined zinc cap with shoulder rubber ring, which fits a standard mason jar.

1. Before filling jar, fit new rubber ring on shoulder.
2. Fill jar. Wipe rim and rubber ring clean.
3. Screw cap down firmly and turn the cap back ¼ inch.
4. As soon as jar is processed and removed from cooker, screw cap down tightly to complete the seal.

A wire-bail type jar with glass lid and rubber ring.

1. Before filling jar, fit new rubber ring on ledge at top of jar.
2. Fill jar. Wipe rim and rubber ring clean.
3. Press glass lid on rubber ring. Pull long wire over lid, fitting it into the groove on lid. Leave short wire up.
4. As soon as jar is processed and removed from cooker, push short wire down to complete the seal.

metal lid and screw band   lined zinc cap with rubber ring   wire-bail jar with rubber ring

Pressure Canning Meats and Fish

1. Before beginning any pressure canning, be sure to read Pressure Canning Directions, page 114.
2. All freshly killed meats and fish should be thoroughly cooled and cleaned before canning.
3. Meats may be canned with or without salt, depending on your flavor preference. If you wish to use salt, add ¼ teaspoon to each half-pint jar, ½ teaspoon to each pint jar and 1 teaspoon to each quart jar.
4. Meats and fish should be processed at 10 pounds pressure. But at altitudes of 2000 feet or higher, use 15 pounds pressure instead of 10.

Food	Instructions	Pounds Pressure	Minutes to Process Half-pints, pints	Quarts
Beef, Veal, Lamb, Pork	Cook until medium done or until center shows almost no pink. Cut up. Fill jars. Pour in boiling broth or water, leaving 1-inch headspace.	10	75	90
Pork Chops, Ham	Fry until brown. Fill jars. Pour in boiling broth or water, leaving 1-inch headspace.	10	75	90
Chicken	Disjoint. Cook with liquid until medium done. Remove bones if desired. Fill jars. Pour in boiling cooking liquid, leaving 1-inch headspace.	10	65 (75 if boneless)	75 (90 if boneless)
Fried Chicken	Disjoint. Fry in hot fat until lightly browned. Fill jars. Pour in boiling broth or water, leaving 1-inch headspace.	10	65	75
Duck, Turkey, Rabbit	Follow directions for Chicken.			
Soup Stock	Make stock (pages 16-18). Skim fat. Pour hot into jars, leaving ½-inch headspace.	10	20	25
Fish (except Salmon)	Cut up. Precook. Remove skin and bones if desired. Fill jars, leaving 1-inch headspace. To tuna add 2 tablespoons oil.	10	100	
Salmon (whole)	Slowly pour hot water on fish, being careful not to break the skin. Scrape skin gently until it is white and clear. Wipe dry. Cut fish crosswise into steaks. Do not remove backbone sections. Fill jars, leaving 1-inch headspace.	10	100	
Clams	Steam to open. Remove from shells. Boil clams in salted water to cover for 5 minutes. Drain. Rinse. Fill jars. Pour in hot weak brine (1 teaspoon salt to 1 quart water), leaving 1-inch headspace.	10	90	90
Shrimp	Boil 7 to 8 minutes in heavy brine to cover (1 gallon water to 1 pound of salt). Drain, shell and devein. Fill jars. Pour in hot weak brine (1 teaspoon salt to 1 quart water), leaving ½-inch headspace.	10	90	90

Pressure Canning Vegetables

1. Before beginning any pressure canning, be sure to read Pressure Canning Directions, page 114.

2. Vegetables may be canned with or without salt, depending on your flavor preference. If you wish to use salt, add ¼ teaspoon to each half-pint jar, ½ teaspoon to each pint jar and 1 teaspoon to each quart jar.

3. Most vegetables can be processed raw. Pack tightly because they shrink during processing. (Exceptions: corn, lima beans and peas must be packed loosely because they expand.) Cover with boiling water, leaving amount of headspace indicated in chart. Process same length of time as cooked vegetables.

4. Most vegetables should be processed at 10 pounds pressure. But at altitudes of 2000 feet or higher, use 15 instead of 10. Exceptions: sauerkraut and tomatoes should be processed at 5 pounds; at 2000 feet process at 10.

Food	Instructions	Pounds Pressure	Minutes to Process Half-pints, pints	Quarts
Asparagus	Trim off scale. Cook 2 minutes in boiling water to cover. Fill jars. Pour in boiling water. Or pack raw and pour in boiling water. Leave ½-inch headspace.	10	25	30
Beans, Lima (fresh)	Shell. Bring to a boil in water to cover. Remove from heat. Fill jars loosely. Pour in boiling water. Or pack raw and pour in boiling water. Leave 1-inch headspace in pints, 1½-inch headspace in quarts.	10	40	50
Beans, Green or Wax	String. Cut up. Boil 5 minutes in water to cover. Fill jars. Pour in boiling water. Or pack raw and pour in boiling water. Leave ½-inch headspace.	10	20	25
Beets	Cut off root and top except retain 1 inch stem. Pressure-cook according to directions in manufacturer's handbook for 6 minutes only. Cut skinned beets into ½-inch slices. Fill jars. Pour in boiling water, leaving ½-inch headspace.	10	30	35
Carrots	Scrape. Slice. Boil 5 minutes in water to cover. Fill jars. Pour in boiling water, leaving ½-inch headspace. Or pack raw and pour in boiling water, leaving 1-inch headspace.	10	25	30
Corn (cream style)	Remove husks. Cut kernels from cob at about center of kernel. Scrape cobs. To each quart of kernels add 1 pint boiling water. Boil 1 minute. Fill jars loosely. Or pack raw and pour in boiling water. Leave 1-inch headspace.	10	95	
Corn (whole kernel)	Remove husks. Cut kernels from cob. To each quart of kernels add 1 pint boiling water and 1 teaspoon salt. Boil 1 minute. Fill jars loosely. Pour in boiling water. Or pack raw and pour in boiling water. Leave 1-inch headspace.	10	55	85
Greens	Use only very fresh tender greens. Wash carefully. Remove tough stems. Bring to boil in small amount of water. Remove from heat. Fill jars loosely. Pour in boiling water, leaving ½-inch headspace.	10	70	90

Food	Instructions	Pounds Pressure	Minutes to Process	
			Half-pints, pints	Quarts
Mushrooms	Trim. Soak in cold water 10 minutes. Cut large ones in half. Boil gently in small amount of water 15 minutes. Fill jars. Pour in boiling water, leaving ½-inch headspace.	10	30	
Okra	Trim ends. Boil 1 minute in water to cover. Cut into 1-inch lengths. Fill jars. Pour in boiling water, leaving ½-inch headspace.	10	25	40
Peas (fresh Black-eye, Cowpeas, Black-eye Beans)	Shell. Bring to a boil in water to cover. Remove from heat. Fill jars loosely. Pour in boiling water. Or pack raw peas loosely and pour in boiling water. Leave 1½-inch headspace.	10	35	40
Peas, Green	Use only young fresh peas. Shell. Bring to a boil in water to cover. Remove from heat. Fill jars loosely. Pour in boiling water. Or pack raw peas loosely and pour in boiling water. Leave 1-inch headspace.	10	40	40
Potatoes	Peel and cut into ½-inch cubes. Boil 2 minutes in water to cover. Or use whole potatoes 1 to 2½ inches in diameter and boil 10 minutes. Fill jars and pour in boiling water, leaving ½-inch headspace.	10	35	40
Pumpkin or Hubbard Squash	Peel and cut into 1-inch cubes. Pressure-cook according to directions in manufacturer's handbook. Drain and puree. Add boiling water to pulp if too thick. Fill jars, leaving 1-inch headspace.	10	65	80
Sauerkraut	Use well-fermented sauerkraut. Bring to a simmer. Remove from heat. Fill jars. Pour in boiling juice, leaving ½-inch headspace.	5	10	15
Squash, Summer (Pattypan, Scalloped, Zucchini)	Trim ends but do not peel. Cut into ½-inch slices. Boil 1-2 minutes in water to cover. Fill jars. Pour in boiling water. Or pack raw and pour in boiling water. Leave ½-inch headspace.	10	30	40
Sweet Potatoes	Boil in water to cover until skins slip off easily. Cut up. Fill jars. Pour in boiling water. Or pack dry, without liquid or salt. Leave 1-inch headspace.	10	55 (wet) 65 (dry)	90 (wet) 95 (dry)
Tomatoes	Dip tomatoes into scalding water, then into cold water. Slip off skins. Cut into quarters. Fill jars tightly. Add juice or boiling water if tomatoes do not make enough liquid. Or bring peeled, quartered tomatoes to a boil in water to cover; remove from heat and pack. Add liquid if necessary. Leave ½-inch headspace.	5	10	10
Tomato Juice	Bring tomatoes to a boil in water to cover. Cook until soft; drain and put through a food press. Season and bring to a boil. Remove from heat. Pour into jars, leaving ½-inch headspace.	5	10	10

Some strong-flavored vegetables like broccoli, Brussels sprouts, cabbage, cauliflower and rutabagas are not recommended for canning.

Pressure Canning Fruits

1. Before beginning any pressure canning, be sure to read Pressure Canning Directions, page 114.
2. To keep peeled fruit from darkening before it is packed, place it in water to which lemon juice or ascorbic acid has been added. Ascorbic acid products can be obtained at drug stores.
3. Pack raw fruits tightly because they shrink during processing.

4. Fruits may be canned with boiling water as the liquid instead of syrup, although sugar does help canned fruit retain its shape, color and flavor.
5. Time processing very carefully because fruits are easily overcooked.
6. Fruits should be processed at 5 pounds pressure. But at altitudes of 2000 feet or higher, use 10 instead of 5.

Food	Instructions	Pounds Pressure	Minutes to Process Half-pints, pints	Quarts
Apples	Peel, core and cut up. Fill jars. Pour in boiling syrup. Or precook 3 minutes in boiling syrup, fill jars and pour in syrup. Leave ½-inch headspace.	5	10	10
Applesauce	Fill jars with hot applesauce (do not cook in cooker), leaving ½-inch headspace.	5	15	15
Apricots, Nectarines	Use whole or cut in half and remove pits. Fill jars. Pour in boiling syrup, leaving ½-inch headspace.	5	10	10
Berries (except Strawberries)	Stem. Fill jars. Pour in boiling syrup, leaving ½-inch headspace.	5	8	8
Cherries	Stem and pit. Fill jars. Pour in boiling syrup, leaving ½-inch headspace.	5	10	10
Figs	Retain stems. Boil 2 minutes in water to cover. Prepare thin syrup from this cooking liquid. Boil figs in syrup for 5 minutes. Fill jars. Add to jars 1½ teaspoons lemon juice per pint or 1 tablespoon per quart. Pour in boiling syrup, leaving ½-inch headspace.	5	10	10
Grapes	Stem. Fill jars. Pour in boiling syrup, leaving 1½-inch headspace.	5	8	8
Peaches	Dip peaches into boiling water, then into cold water. Slip off skins. Cut in half and remove pits. Fill jars. Pour in boiling syrup, leaving ½-inch headspace.	5	10	10
Pears	Peel, cut in half and core. Fill jars. Pour in boiling syrup, leaving ½-inch headspace.	5	10	10
Pineapple	Peel, remove eyes, slice and core. Boil 5-10 minutes in medium syrup to cover. Fill jars. Pour in boiling syrup, leaving ½-inch headspace.	5	15	15
Plums	Prick skins. Fill jars. Pour in boiling syrup, leaving ½-inch headspace.	5	10	10
Rhubarb	Cut into pieces. Fill jars. Pour in boiling syrup. Or cook rhubarb (do not use pressure cooker) and fill jars with rhubarb sauce. Leave ½-inch headspace.	5	5	5

tip

For thin syrup: Bring to a boil 3 parts water or juice and 1 part sugar. Use with soft fruits such as sweet cherries and berries.

For medium syrup: Bring to a boil 2 parts water or juice and 1 part sugar. Use with peaches, pears, sour berries, acid fruits.

For heavy syrup: Bring to a boil 1 part water or juice and 1 part sugar. Use with larger sour fruits that you wish to make extra sweet.

Tips for Canners

- The pressure canning directions and recipes in this chapter are based on the standard procedures and processing times developed by the U.S. Department of Agriculture. Follow pressure canning directions exactly. Do not improvise shortcuts.

- These canning directions are for use with a weight-control canner. (If you have a dial-gauge canner, follow the directions provided by the manufacturer.)

- The control on a weight-control canner never needs to be tested because it cannot get out of order. Dial-gauge canners need to be tested once a year for accuracy.

- Before canning, sort fruits and vegetables by size and ripeness. They will look and taste better.

- To can a mixture of foods, like soup or stew, process for length of time required by the ingredient that has the longest processing time.

- The U.S. Department of Agriculture states that unless you are absolutely sure of your canning methods, boil food at least 10 minutes before using. (Boil corn and spinach 20 minutes.)

Russian Vegetable Salad

2 quarts water
1 tablespoon salt
1 teaspoon sugar
1 teaspoon mixed pickling spice
3 cups diced peeled potatoes (½-inch dice)
3 cups diced peeled turnips (½-inch dice)
3 cups diced carrots (½-inch dice)
3 cups fresh peas

1. Follow Steps 1 through 5 of Pressure Canning Directions.
2. Add water, salt, sugar and pickling spice to cooker. Bring brine to a boil. Reduce heat. Add potatoes, turnips and carrots and blanch, uncovered, 5 minutes. Drain and reserve liquid. Set aside potatoes, turnips and carrots.
3. Pour reserved liquid into cooker and bring back to a boil. Reduce heat. Add peas and blanch, uncovered, 1½ minutes. Drain and reserve liquid.
4. Mix all vegetables until evenly combined. Spoon into six 1-pint canning jars, leaving ½-inch headspace between food and closure. Cover vegetables with hot blanching liquid, retaining ½-inch headspace.
5. Follow Steps 7 through 10 of Pressure Canning Directions.
6. Cover cooker, set control at 10 and place over high heat until control jiggles. Reduce heat and cook 40 minutes.
7. Finish according to Steps 12 through 17 of Pressure Canning Directions.

Six 1-pint jars (6- to 22-quart cooker).

Asparagus and Peppers Vinaigrette

5 dozen asparagus spears, washed
6 red peppers, seeded and cut into
   thin strips.
2 cups oil (preferably olive oil)
⅔ cup vinegar
1 teaspoon salt
¼ teaspoon pepper
   Pinch of sugar
6 cloves garlic, peeled

1. Snap off tough ends of asparagus, making stalks of uniform length that will fit your canning jars. Peel any tough fibrous skin.
2. Follow Steps 1 through 5 of Pressure Canning Directions.
3. Divide asparagus spears and pepper slices among six 1-pint canning jars. Mix together oil, vinegar, salt, pepper and sugar and pour over vegetables, leaving ½-inch headspace between liquid and closure. Place 1 garlic clove in each jar.
4. Follow Steps 7 through 10 of Pressure Canning Directions.
5. Cover cooker, set control at 10 and place over high heat until control jiggles. Reduce heat and cook 25 minutes.
6. Finish according to Steps 12 through 17 of Pressure Canning Directions.

Six 1-pint jars (6- to 22-quart cooker).

Zucchini, Italian Style

4 pounds zucchini, scrubbed
1 quart water
1 teaspoon salt
   Pinch of sugar
4 pounds ripe, red tomatoes,
   washed and stemmed
½ cup olive oil
1 medium onion, coarsely chopped
6 cloves garlic, minced
2 teaspoons salt
1 teaspoon basil
½ teaspoon each pepper, oregano
   and thyme
6 bay leaves

1. Trim zucchini and cut into spears ½ inch shorter than the height of your canning jars and ½ inch thick.
2. Follow Steps 1 through 5 of Pressure Canning Directions.
3. Add water, salt and sugar to cooker. Bring brine to a boil. Reduce heat. Add zucchini spears and blanch, uncovered, 1 minute. Drain and reserve liquid.
4. Pack zucchini loosely into six 1-pint canning jars.
5. Pour reserved liquid into cooker and bring back to a boil. Reduce heat. Add tomatoes and blanch, uncovered, 30 seconds. Drain and discard liquid. Refresh tomatoes under cold running water until cool. Peel, seed and coarsely chop the pulp; reserve.
6. Heat oil in cooker. Sauté onion and garlic, stirring, until the onion is translucent. Add tomatoes, salt, basil, pepper, oregano and thyme. Cook, stirring occasionally, 20 minutes.
7. Place a bay leaf in each of the canning jars and fill with the hot tomato sauce, leaving ½-inch headspace between liquid and closure.
8. Follow Steps 7 through 10 of Pressure Canning Directions.
9. Cover cooker, set control at 10 and place over high heat until control jiggles. Reduce heat and cook 30 minutes.
10. Finish according to Steps 12 through 17 of Pressure Canning Directions.

Six 1-pint jars (6- to 22-quart cooker).

Dilly Beans

3 pounds green beans
4 quarts water
4 tablespoons salt
4 cups vinegar
1 cup sugar
2 tablespoons mixed pickling spice
2 cloves garlic, minced
1 cup fresh dill weed, coarsely
   chopped

1. Wash beans well and snip off ends, leaving whole beans a size that fits your canning jars. Soak in ice water for 30 minutes.
2. Follow Steps 1 through 5 of Pressure Canning Directions.
3. Add water and salt to cooker. Bring brine to a boil. Reduce heat. Add green beans and blanch, uncovered, 10 minutes. Drain and discard liquid.
4. Pack six 1-pint canning jars loosely with blanched green beans. Combine vinegar, sugar, pickling spice and garlic and pour over beans, leaving ½-inch headspace between liquid and closure. Sprinkle with dill.
5. Follow Steps 7 through 10 of Pressure Canning Directions.
6. Cover cooker, set control at 10 and place over high heat until control jiggles. Reduce heat and cook 5 minutes.
7. Finish according to Steps 12 through 17 of Pressure Canning Directions.

Six 1-pint jars (6- to 22-quart cooker).

Fresh Tomato Sauce

6 pounds fresh tomatoes, peeled,
   seeded and coarsely chopped
1 large Spanish onion, minced
1 cup tomato paste
1 teaspoon each salt and sugar
1 tablespoon lemon juice
1 teaspoon each basil, oregano and
   thyme
2 cloves garlic, minced

1. Combine all ingredients and mix well until evenly blended.
2. Follow Steps 1 through 5 of Pressure Canning Directions.
3. Spoon tomato mixture into six 1-pint jars, leaving ½-inch headspace between food and closure.
4. Follow Steps 7 through 10 of Pressure Canning Directions.
5. Cover cooker, set control at 10 and place over high heat until control jiggles. Reduce heat and cook 15 minutes.
6. Finish according to Steps 12 through 17 of Pressure Canning Directions.

Six 1-pint jars (6- to 22-quart cooker).

tip

You can use your uncovered cooker for blanching or pre-cooking, if you wish. Or use another suitable cooking pot and keep the cooker ready for processing the filled jars.

Index

Index

Ground beef (continued)
spaghetti and meatballs, 48
stuffed cabbage, 46
stuffed green peppers, 11
stuffed summer squash, 81

Ham
canning, 117
chicken roll-ups, 70
fresh, in beer, 73
jambalaya, 74
meatball soup, 21
Hamburger. See GROUND BEEF
Hearty fish soup, 61
Hors d'oeuvres. See APPETIZERS

Indian pudding, New England, 99
Individual meat loaves, 10
Italian sauce, quick, 11

Jambalaya, 74

Kale, 13
Kasha varnishkas, 44
Kidney, steak and,
pie, 38
stew, 38
Kidney beans, 26
beans with beef, 29
prize-winning chili, 28
Knockwurst
choucroute garni, 72

Lamb
and lima beans, 50
canning, 117
cassoulet, 27
chops
curried, 59
Lancashire hot pot, 41
curries for a crowd, 70
curry, 41
shanks, lemon, 50
Lancashire hot pot, 41
Leeks
cock-a-leekie, 22
Lemon-baked chicken, 60
Lemon lamb shanks, 50
Lemon sauce, 97
Lentil(s), 26
casserole, 52
Light fruitcake, 100
Lima beans (dried), 26
beans with beef, 29
lamb and, 50
Lima beans (fresh)
canning, 118
soupe au pistou, 24
Liver, pork
pâté maison, 69
Lobster tails, 61

Marmalade
amber, 88
carrot, 88

Marmalade soufflé, 65
Mashed potatoes, 11
Matzoh ball soup, 20
Meat. See also specific kind
canning, 117
Meat loaf, 47
meatless, 84
Meat loaves, individual, 10
Meat sauce for spaghetti, 48
Meatball(s)
soup, 21
spaghetti and, 48
stew, 47
Meatless meat loaf, 84
Mellow old-fashioned oats, 32
Mocha custard, 107
Mush, cornmeal, 31
Mushrooms
almond-stuffed, 64
broccoli and, 77
canning, 119
vegetable platter, 84
Mussels
cioppino, 24
Mustard sauce, 44

Navy pea beans, 26
Boston baked beans, 27
Nectarines, canning, 120
New England boiled dinner plus, 71
New England clam chowder, 23
New England Indian pudding, 99
New York clam chowder, 23

Oats
cereal blend, 32
meatless meat loaf, 84
mellow old-fashioned, 32
steel, super, 32
Okra
canning, 119
Creole, 79
Onions
creamed white, Williamsburg, 79
potatoes and, 12
Orange(s)
amber marmalade, 88
beets, 76
candied fruit peel, 108
custard in orange cups, 106
Oxtail ragout Seville, 42

Paella Valenciana, 43
Parsley potatoes, steamed, 11
Parsnips, glazed, 79
Pâté maison, 69
Pea beans, navy, 26
Boston baked beans, 27
Pea pods, Chinese
vegetable platter, 84
Peach(es)
brandied, 103
canning, 120
dried, preserve, 87
glazed, 103
stewed, 66

Pears
brandied, 103
canning, 120
in red wine, 103
stuffed, 104
Peas, green
canning, 119
vegetable platter, 84
Peppers
asparagus and, vinaigrette, 122
beef and, Chinese, 38
chutney, 86
ratatouille, 83
stuffed green, 11
Pickle, watermelon, 87
Pie
caramel fruit, 107
steak and kidney, 38
Pineapple, canning, 120
Pink beans, 26
Pinto beans, 26
Southwestern pintos, 28
Plum pudding, Dickens', 100
Plums
canning, 120
prune-, al vino, 104
Poached turkey breast, 51
Poached turkey legs, 51
Pommes Anna, 10
Pompano royale, 63
Pork
and cumin hors d'oeuvres,
Spanish, 69
canning, 117
cassoulet, 27
chops, 12
canning, 117
choucroute garni, 72
cider buffet loaf, 68
meatball soup, 21
pâté maison, 69
sausage. See SAUSAGE(S)
spareribs
Chinese, 41
glazed, 68
Pot roast, quick, 11
Potato(es)
and onions, 12
and turnip soup, 22
"baked," 80
canning, 119
green beans and, 76
mashed, 11
pommes Anna, 10
puff, codfish, 52
scalloped, 80
steamed parsley, 11
sweet. See SWEET POTATO(ES)
Potted beef brisket, 46
Preserve(s), 86–88
amber marmalade, 88
apricot and date chutney, 86
carrot marmalade, 88
chutney, 86
dried apricot, 87
dried peach, 87
red tomato chutney, 86
watermelon pickle, 87
Pressure canning. See CANNING
Pressure cooking, general
information, 6–8